Practical Data Science with R

Build Machine Learning Models and Data Visualizations with R

Greyson Chesterfield

COPYRIGHT

DISCLAIMER

The information provided in this book is for general informational purposes only. All content in this book reflects the author's views and is based on their research, knowledge, and experiences. The author and publisher make no representations or warranties of any kind concerning the completeness, accuracy, reliability, suitability, or availability of the information contained herein.

This book is not intended to be a substitute for professional advice, diagnosis, or treatment. Readers should seek professional advice for any specific concerns or conditions. The author and publisher disclaim any liability or responsibility for any direct, indirect, incidental, or consequential loss or damage arising from the use of the information contained in this book.

Contents

Chapter 1: Introduction to Data Science and R

1.1 Overview of Data Science in Practical Terms

Data science, at its core, is the art and science of extracting valuable insights from data. It is not just a buzzword but a transformative discipline that combines elements of mathematics, statistics, programming, and domain expertise. Businesses, governments, and researchers increasingly rely on data-driven decisions to innovate, optimize, and predict future trends. But what exactly does this mean in practice?

What Does a Data Scientist Do?

In simple terms, a data scientist works with data to answer questions or solve problems. Here are some everyday examples:

- **E-commerce platforms** use data science to recommend products based on customer preferences and past purchases.

- **Healthcare organizations** analyze patient data to predict disease outbreaks or recommend personalized treatments.

- **Retail chains** optimize inventory levels and forecast demand using predictive analytics.

- **Social media platforms** utilize data science to filter spam, recommend content, or identify trending topics.

In practice, data science involves:

1. **Defining the Problem**: Identifying what you aim to achieve or understand from the data.

2. **Data Collection**: Gathering data from various sources, such as databases, APIs, or web scraping.

3. **Data Cleaning and Preprocessing**: Preparing the raw data by handling missing values, duplicates, or inconsistencies.

4. **Exploratory Data Analysis (EDA)**: Understanding the data through visualization and summary statistics.

5. **Modeling**: Applying machine learning or statistical methods to make predictions or extract patterns.

6. **Communicating Results**: Presenting findings through dashboards, visualizations, or reports to stakeholders.

1.2 Why R is Ideal for Data Science

As a data scientist, choosing the right tool is essential. While there are many programming languages and tools available, R has established itself as one of the most versatile and powerful tools for data science.

1.2.1 What is R?

R is an open-source programming language specifically designed for data analysis, statistics, and visualization. Created in the 1990s, it has since grown into a globally recognized platform with a vibrant community of developers and contributors. Its ecosystem is enriched by an expansive library of packages that simplify data manipulation, visualization, and machine learning.

1.2.2 Key Advantages of R

1. **Statistical Excellence**: R was created by statisticians for statisticians. It offers unparalleled support for statistical modeling, hypothesis testing, and probability analysis.

2. **Rich Visualization Capabilities**: With libraries like ggplot2, lattice, and plotly, R allows for the creation of high-quality, customizable visualizations.

3. **Comprehensive Ecosystem**: The CRAN repository provides thousands of packages that extend R's functionality, from time series forecasting to natural language processing.

4. **Flexibility**: R can handle structured and unstructured data, making it ideal for diverse data science tasks.

5. **Integration**: It integrates seamlessly with databases (e.g., MySQL, PostgreSQL), big data tools (e.g., Spark), and other programming languages (e.g., Python, C++).

6. **Community Support**: R has an active community of users and developers who contribute tutorials, forums, and open-source projects.

7. **Reproducible Research**: R Markdown and RStudio make it easy to create reproducible reports, combining code, output, and text in a single document.

1.2.3 R vs. Other Programming Languages

While Python and R are often compared for data science, each has its strengths. R is typically favored for its:

- **Focus on statistics**: It's purpose-built for advanced statistical analysis.

- **Simplicity in visualization**: ggplot2 is regarded as one of the best tools for creating data visualizations.

- **Quick prototyping**: With its extensive library of built-in functions, prototyping models and visualizations is faster in R.

1.3 Setting Up the R Environment and Essential Packages

Before diving into data science projects, it's essential to set up your R environment. Here's a step-by-step guide to getting started.

1.3.1 Installing R

1. **Download R**: Go to the Comprehensive R Archive Network (CRAN) website at https://cran.r-project.org.

2. **Select Your Operating System**: Download the appropriate installer for your operating system (Windows, macOS, or Linux).

3. **Follow the Installation Instructions**: Run the installer and follow the prompts to complete the installation.

1.3.2 Installing RStudio

RStudio is a powerful Integrated Development Environment (IDE) for R that simplifies coding, debugging, and visualization.

1. **Download RStudio**: Visit https://www.rstudio.com and download the free RStudio Desktop version.

2. **Install RStudio**: Run the installer and set it up on your system.

1.3.3 Installing Essential Packages

R's capabilities are greatly enhanced by packages. Some essential packages for data science include:

- **tidyverse**: A collection of packages (dplyr, ggplot2, tidyr, readr) for data manipulation and visualization.

- **caret**: Simplifies the process of building and evaluating machine learning models.

- **data.table**: Provides fast and efficient data manipulation tools.

- **shiny**: Enables the creation of interactive web apps.

- **ggplot2**: For high-quality data visualizations.

- **forecast**: For time series analysis and forecasting.

How to Install Packages in R

You can install packages directly from CRAN using the install.packages() function. For example:

R

```
install.packages("tidyverse")
```

Once installed, load the package into your session using the library() function:

R

```
library(tidyverse)
```

1.3.4 Creating Your First R Script

1. Open RStudio and create a new script file (File > New File > R Script).

2. Write and execute your first lines of code. For example:

R

```
# Hello, R!

message <- "Welcome to the world of Data Science with R"

print(message)
```

3. Save your script and experiment with basic commands.

1.3.5 Setting Up a Project

Using projects in RStudio helps organize your work. Here's how to set one up:

1. **Create a New Project**: Go to File > New Project.

2. **Choose a Directory**: Create a new folder or use an existing one.

3. **Organize Your Files**: Save data files, scripts, and outputs in structured folders.

1.3.6 Getting Comfortable with the RStudio Interface

The RStudio interface is divided into four main panes:

1. **Source Pane**: Where you write your scripts.

2. **Console**: Displays code execution results.

3. **Environment/History Pane**: Tracks variables and command history.

4. **Files/Plots/Packages/Help Pane**: Helps navigate files, view plots, manage packages, and access documentation.

This chapter introduced you to the fundamentals of data science, explained why R is a preferred tool, and guided you through setting up your R environment. By now, you should have a basic understanding of data science's real-world applications, the strengths of R, and how to get started with RStudio and essential packages.

Chapter 2: Data Manipulation with R

2.1 Introduction to tidyverse for Data Manipulation

Data manipulation is one of the most critical steps in the data science workflow. Raw data often contains inconsistencies, irrelevant information, or missing values that must be addressed before analysis. R, with its powerful tidyverse ecosystem, provides a suite of tools to make data manipulation both intuitive and efficient.

What is the tidyverse?

The tidyverse is a collection of R packages designed for data science. Developed by Hadley Wickham and the RStudio team, the tidyverse simplifies common tasks such as data cleaning, transformation, and visualization. The core packages in the tidyverse include:

- **dplyr**: For data manipulation (e.g., filtering, summarizing).
- **tidyr**: For reshaping and tidying data.
- **readr**: For importing data files.

- **ggplot2**: For visualization (covered in later chapters).

- **tibble**: For working with data frames.

The tidyverse follows a consistent syntax and philosophy of "tidy data," where:

1. Each variable forms a column.

2. Each observation forms a row.

3. Each type of observational unit forms a table.

This consistency makes it easy to apply a series of operations on data seamlessly.

The Power of the Pipe Operator (%>%)

One of the most useful features of tidyverse is the **pipe operator (%>%)** from the magrittr package. It allows you to chain multiple operations together in a readable format. For example:

R

```
data %>%
  filter(condition) %>%
  mutate(new_column = transformation) %>%
  summarize(summary_stat = mean(column))
```

2.2 Real-World Examples: Cleaning Survey Data and Reshaping Formats

Let's explore how to use tidyverse packages for data cleaning and reshaping with real-world examples.

2.2.1 Cleaning Survey Data

Consider a scenario where you've collected survey data, but it needs cleaning before analysis. Here's an example dataset:

R

```r
survey_data <- data.frame(
  Name = c("Alice", "Bob", "Charlie", "Alice", "Bob"),
  Age = c(25, NA, 35, 25, NA),
  Gender = c("F", "M", "M", "F", "M"),
  Response = c("Yes", "No", "Yes", "Yes", "No")
)
```

Step 1: Identifying Duplicates

Using dplyr::distinct():

R

```r
cleaned_data <- survey_data %>%
  distinct()
```

Step 2: Renaming Columns

Using dplyr::rename() to make column names more meaningful:

R

```
cleaned_data <- cleaned_data %>%
  rename(
    Participant_Name = Name,
    Participant_Age = Age
  )
```

Step 3: Filtering Incomplete Records

Using dplyr::filter() to remove rows with missing ages:

R

```
filtered_data <- cleaned_data %>%
  filter(!is.na(Participant_Age))
```

2.2.2 Reshaping Data Formats

Data often comes in formats that aren't suitable for analysis. The tidyr package makes it easy to reshape data into tidy formats.

Example: Wide to Long Format

Consider the following wide-format dataset:

R

```r
grades <- data.frame(
  Student = c("Alice", "Bob", "Charlie"),
  Math = c(90, 85, 78),
  Science = c(88, 92, 95)
)
```

Transform it into a long format using tidyr::pivot_longer():

R

```r
long_grades <- grades %>%
  pivot_longer(cols = Math:Science,
               names_to = "Subject",
               values_to = "Score")
```

Example: Long to Wide Format

Conversely, convert the long format back to wide using tidyr::pivot_wider():

R

```r
wide_grades <- long_grades %>%
```

```
pivot_wider(names_from = Subject, values_from =
Score)
```

These transformations allow flexibility depending on
your analysis needs.

2.3 Handling Missing Data

Missing data is inevitable in real-world datasets and
can pose significant challenges for analysis. R offers
several tools for detecting, visualizing, and handling
missing values.

2.3.1 Detecting Missing Values

The first step in handling missing data is identifying
where it exists. In R, NA represents missing values.

Checking for Missing Values

Use is.na() to detect missing values:

R

```
sum(is.na(survey_data$Age))  # Count missing
values in the Age column
```

2.3.2 Strategies for Handling Missing Data

  1. **Remove Missing Data**: Drop rows or columns
     with missing values using tidyr::drop_na():

R

```
complete_data <- survey_data %>%

 drop_na(Age)
```

2. **Impute Missing Data**: Replace missing values with an estimate using tidyr::replace_na():

R

```
imputed_data <- survey_data %>%

 mutate(Age = replace_na(Age,
median(survey_data$Age, na.rm = TRUE)))
```

3. **Flag Missing Data**: Create an indicator column to mark rows with missing values:

R

```
flagged_data <- survey_data %>%

 mutate(Missing_Age = if_else(is.na(Age), TRUE,
FALSE))
```

2.3.3 Visualizing Missing Data

The naniar package provides tools to visualize missing data patterns:

R

```
library(naniar)

gg_miss_var(survey_data)  # Visualize the number of
missing values per column
```

By visualizing missing data, you can better decide how to handle it.

2.4 Real-World Case Study: Data Cleaning and Transformation

Let's apply these techniques to a more comprehensive example. Imagine you've been provided the following messy dataset:

R

```
sales_data <- data.frame(
  Order_ID = c(101, 102, 103, 104, 105),
  Customer_Name = c("Alice", "Bob", "Charlie", "Dana", NA),
  Product = c("Laptop", "Phone", "Tablet", NA, "Phone"),
  Price = c(1000, 500, 300, 700, NA),
  Quantity = c(1, 2, 1, 1, 3)
)
```

Step 1: Inspect and Summarize the Data

R

```
summary(sales_data)
```

Step 2: Remove Rows with Critical Missing Information

If an order lacks a customer name or product, it's considered invalid:

R

```
sales_data <- sales_data %>%

  drop_na(Customer_Name, Product)
```

Step 3: Fill Missing Prices

Impute missing prices with the median of available prices:

R

```
sales_data <- sales_data %>%

  mutate(Price = replace_na(Price, median(Price, na.rm = TRUE)))
```

Step 4: Add Total Sales Column

Calculate the total sales for each order:

R

```
sales_data <- sales_data %>%

  mutate(Total_Sales = Price * Quantity)
```

Step 5: Summarize Sales by Product

Aggregate total sales by product:

R

```
sales_summary <- sales_data %>%
  group_by(Product) %>%
  summarize(Total_Sales = sum(Total_Sales, na.rm = TRUE))
```

The final cleaned dataset is now ready for analysis and visualization.

This chapter introduced you to the tidyverse for data manipulation, focusing on dplyr and tidyr to clean and reshape data. You learned how to handle real-world issues like duplicates, messy formats, and missing values. By mastering these tools and techniques, you can prepare raw data for insightful analysis.

Chapter 3: Data Exploration and Summarization

3.1 The Role of Data Exploration in Data Science

Before delving into modeling or visualization, a crucial step in any data science workflow is **data exploration**. Data exploration allows you to:

1. Understand the structure and content of your dataset.

2. Identify patterns, trends, and potential outliers.

3. Detect data quality issues, such as missing or inconsistent values.

4. Formulate hypotheses and guide further analysis.

The aim of this chapter is to provide hands-on guidance on exploring and summarizing datasets using R's powerful tools, particularly the dplyr package. We will also explore how to profile data distributions and analyze customer demographics in a practical case study.

3.2 Descriptive Statistics with dplyr

The **dplyr** package is part of the tidyverse and is known for its intuitive, user-friendly syntax for data manipulation and summarization. It provides a suite of functions that make calculating descriptive statistics—such as mean, median, standard deviation, and quantiles—straightforward.

3.2.1 Understanding Descriptive Statistics

Descriptive statistics summarize and describe the main features of a dataset. Here are some key measures:

- **Central Tendency**: Mean, median, and mode.

- **Dispersion**: Range, interquartile range (IQR), variance, and standard deviation.

- **Shape**: Skewness and kurtosis to understand the distribution's asymmetry and peakedness.

3.2.2 Key dplyr Functions for Summarization

Here are some commonly used functions for summarizing data:

- summarize(): Generates summary statistics for a dataset.

- group_by(): Groups data for aggregated calculations.

- mutate(): Adds new columns based on existing ones.

- filter(): Subsets rows based on conditions.

- arrange(): Orders rows.

3.2.3 Example: Summarizing Sales Data

Let's analyze a sample dataset containing sales data:

R

```r
library(dplyr)


# Sample dataset
sales_data <- data.frame(
  Product = c("A", "B", "A", "C", "B", "A", "C", "C"),
  Sales = c(100, 200, 150, 300, 250, 120, 330, 310),
  Region = c("North", "South", "East", "North", "East", "South", "North", "South")
)


# Calculate descriptive statistics
summary_stats <- sales_data %>%
  group_by(Product) %>%
  summarize(
    Total_Sales = sum(Sales),
```

```
Average_Sales = mean(Sales),

Median_Sales = median(Sales),

Sales_SD = sd(Sales)

)


print(summary_stats)
```

This script calculates total, average, median, and standard deviation of sales for each product, helping identify which products perform consistently or have significant variability.

3.3 Data Profiling and Understanding Distributions

Data profiling involves examining datasets in detail to assess their structure, quality, and statistical properties. It is critical for detecting anomalies and ensuring the data is ready for further analysis.

3.3.1 Visualizing Distributions

Visualizing data distributions helps you grasp the spread and shape of your data at a glance. Key visualization methods include:

1. **Histograms**: Show frequency distributions for numeric variables.

2. **Box Plots**: Highlight the median, quartiles, and potential outliers.

3. **Density Plots**: Provide a smoothed estimate of the distribution.

Example: Visualizing Customer Age Distribution

Let's analyze the distribution of customer ages:

R

```r
library(ggplot2)


# Sample data
customer_data <- data.frame(
  CustomerID = 1:100,
  Age = sample(18:70, 100, replace = TRUE)
)


# Create a histogram
ggplot(customer_data, aes(x = Age)) +
  geom_histogram(binwidth = 5, fill = "blue", alpha = 0.7, color = "black") +
  labs(title = "Age Distribution of Customers", x = "Age", y = "Frequency")
```

This histogram reveals age trends, such as whether most customers fall into a specific age group.

3.3.2 Key Distribution Metrics

- **Skewness**: Measures asymmetry in the data. Positive skew indicates a long tail on the right.

- **Kurtosis**: Measures the "tailedness" of the distribution. High kurtosis indicates more outliers.

Use the moments package to calculate these metrics:

R

```
library(moments)


# Calculate skewness and kurtosis

skewness(customer_data$Age)

kurtosis(customer_data$Age)
```

3.3.3 Identifying Outliers

Outliers can skew results and impact models. Box plots are particularly effective for spotting them.

R

```
# Box plot to identify outliers

ggplot(customer_data, aes(x = "", y = Age)) +

  geom_boxplot(fill = "orange", alpha = 0.7) +
```

```
labs(title = "Box Plot of Customer Ages", x = "", y =
"Age")
```

3.4 Case Study: Analyzing Customer Demographics

Let's put these techniques into practice by analyzing customer demographics for a retail company. The dataset includes information on customer age, gender, region, and total spending.

3.4.1 Step 1: Load and Inspect the Dataset

Start by loading and previewing the dataset:

R

```r
# Sample dataset
customer_data <- data.frame(
  CustomerID = 1:100,
  Age = sample(18:70, 100, replace = TRUE),
  Gender = sample(c("Male", "Female"), 100, replace
= TRUE),
  Region = sample(c("North", "South", "East", "West"),
100, replace = TRUE),
  Spending = runif(100, 50, 500)
)
```

```
# View the first few rows

head(customer_data)
```

3.4.2 Step 2: Summarize Demographics

Group the data by gender and region to understand spending patterns:

R

```
# Summarize spending by gender and region

demographic_summary <- customer_data %>%
  group_by(Gender, Region) %>%
  summarize(
    Average_Age = mean(Age),
    Total_Spending = sum(Spending),
    Average_Spending = mean(Spending)
  )

print(demographic_summary)
```

3.4.3 Step 3: Visualize Findings

1. **Bar Plot of Spending by Region**:

R

```r
ggplot(demographic_summary, aes(x = Region, y =
Total_Spending, fill = Gender)) +

 geom_bar(stat = "identity", position = "dodge") +

 labs(title = "Total Spending by Region and Gender",
x = "Region", y = "Total Spending")
```

2. **Scatter Plot of Age vs. Spending**:

R

```r
ggplot(customer_data, aes(x = Age, y = Spending,
color = Gender)) +

 geom_point(alpha = 0.7) +

 labs(title = "Age vs. Spending by Gender", x = "Age",
y = "Spending")
```

3.4.4 Insights and Actionable Outcomes

Based on the analysis:

- Certain regions may have higher spending trends.

- Male and female customers may exhibit different spending behaviors.

- Age might correlate with spending, indicating potential for targeted marketing.

These insights can guide marketing campaigns, inventory planning, and customer segmentation.

This chapter covered key techniques for data exploration and summarization using dplyr. You learned how to:

- Calculate descriptive statistics.

- Profile data and visualize distributions.

- Identify outliers and trends.

- Analyze customer demographics in a practical case study.

The next chapter will dive into data visualization, helping you turn these insights into compelling visual narratives.

Chapter 4: Data Visualization Basics

4.1 Creating Impactful Charts with ggplot2

Visualization is one of the most crucial aspects of data science, bridging the gap between raw data and actionable insights. ggplot2, part of the tidyverse suite, is one of the most powerful and flexible libraries for data visualization in R. Let's explore how to use it effectively.

4.1.1 The Grammar of Graphics

ggplot2 is built around the "grammar of graphics" concept, which breaks down a plot into layers, enabling you to build visualizations systematically.

- **Data**: The dataset you're visualizing.

- **Aesthetics (aes)**: How data is mapped to visual properties like x-axis, y-axis, color, size, or shape.

- **Geometries (geoms)**: The type of plot, such as points, lines, or bars.

- **Facets**: Breaking data into subplots based on a categorical variable.

- **Scales**: Transforming data for clarity, e.g., logarithmic scaling.

- **Themes**: Adjusting non-data elements, like fonts, backgrounds, and gridlines.

4.1.2 Basic Syntax of ggplot2

A ggplot2 visualization begins with the ggplot() function. Here's a simple example:

R

```
library(ggplot2)


# Sample dataset: mtcars
ggplot(data = mtcars, aes(x = mpg, y = wt)) +
  geom_point() +
  labs(title = "Relationship Between MPG and Weight",
      x = "Miles per Gallon (MPG)",
      y = "Weight (1000 lbs)")
```

This produces a scatterplot showing the relationship between miles per gallon (mpg) and weight (wt) in the mtcars dataset.

4.1.3 Common Chart Types with ggplot2

1. **Scatterplots**

   o Use when exploring relationships between two numerical variables.

   o Example:

R

```
ggplot(data = mtcars, aes(x = hp, y = mpg)) +
  geom_point(aes(color = cyl)) +
  labs(title = "Horsepower vs MPG",
    x = "Horsepower",
    y = "Miles per Gallon")
```

2. **Bar Charts**

   o Ideal for comparing categorical data.

   o Example:

R

```
ggplot(data = mtcars, aes(x = factor(cyl))) +
  geom_bar(fill = "steelblue") +
  labs(title = "Count of Cars by Cylinder",
    x = "Number of Cylinders",
    y = "Count")
```

3. **Line Charts**
   - ○ Great for visualizing trends over time.
   - ○ Example:

R

```r
time_series <- data.frame(
  year = c(2010, 2011, 2012, 2013, 2014),
  sales = c(100, 150, 200, 250, 300)
)

ggplot(data = time_series, aes(x = year, y = sales)) +
  geom_line(color = "darkgreen") +
  geom_point(color = "red") +
  labs(title = "Yearly Sales Growth",
    x = "Year",
    y = "Sales")
```

4. **Histograms**
   - ○ Useful for understanding data distributions.
   - ○ Example:

R

```
ggplot(data = mtcars, aes(x = mpg)) +

  geom_histogram(binwidth = 5, fill = "skyblue", color
= "black") +

  labs(title = "Distribution of Miles per Gallon",

      x = "Miles per Gallon",

      y = "Frequency")
```

5. **Boxplots**
   - Visualize distributions and identify outliers.
   - Example:

R

```
ggplot(data = mtcars, aes(x = factor(cyl), y = mpg)) +

  geom_boxplot(fill = "lightblue") +

  labs(title = "MPG by Cylinder Count",

      x = "Cylinders",

      y = "Miles per Gallon")
```

4.2 Principles of Visual Storytelling

Creating a plot isn't just about technical accuracy; it's also about conveying a clear message to your audience. Here are some principles to guide your storytelling.

4.2.1 Define the Purpose

Before you create a visualization, ask yourself:

- What question are you answering?
- What insight should the viewer take away?

For instance:

- A line chart might highlight a trend in sales over time.
- A bar chart might compare product popularity across categories.

4.2.2 Simplify for Clarity

Cluttered plots confuse rather than clarify. Here's how to avoid that:

- Focus on essential data points.
- Minimize unnecessary elements like excessive gridlines or legends.
- Use consistent color schemes to avoid distraction.

Example:

R

```
ggplot(data = mtcars, aes(x = factor(gear), fill =
factor(cyl))) +
```

```
geom_bar() +

labs(title = "Gear Distribution by Cylinder Count",

    x = "Gears",

    y = "Count") +

theme_minimal()
```

4.2.3 Emphasize Key Insights

Highlight the most critical aspects of your data:

- Use annotations to explain spikes or trends.
- Highlight specific points with color or size adjustments.

Example with annotations:

R

```
ggplot(data = mtcars, aes(x = wt, y = mpg)) +

  geom_point() +

  geom_smooth(method = "lm", color = "blue") +

  annotate("text", x = 5, y = 30, label = "Lighter cars
are more fuel-efficient") +

  labs(title = "Fuel Efficiency by Weight",

     x = "Weight (1000 lbs)",

     y = "Miles per Gallon")
```

4.2.4 Make It Accessible

Ensure that your visualizations are:

- **Legible**: Use clear fonts and appropriately sized labels.

- **Colorblind-friendly**: Opt for accessible color palettes.

- **Self-contained**: Provide enough context (titles, labels, legends) for viewers to interpret the visualization independently.

4.3 Real-World Examples: Visualizing Sales Trends

To bring these concepts together, let's explore a case study: visualizing sales trends for a fictional retail company.

4.3.1 Dataset Overview

The dataset contains the following columns:

- date: Date of transaction.

- sales: Total sales amount.

- category: Product category (e.g., electronics, clothing, home goods).

- region: Sales region (e.g., North, South, East, West).

4.3.2 Monthly Sales Trends

Goal: Analyze monthly sales trends over a year.

Code:

R

```r
# Create example dataset
sales_data <- data.frame(
  date = seq(as.Date("2023-01-01"), as.Date("2023-12-31"), by = "month"),
  sales = c(5000, 5500, 5300, 5700, 6200, 6500, 6800, 7000, 7200, 7100, 6900, 7300)
)

# Line plot
ggplot(data = sales_data, aes(x = date, y = sales)) +
  geom_line(color = "blue") +
  geom_point(color = "red") +
  labs(title = "Monthly Sales Trends in 2023",
       x = "Month",
       y = "Sales ($)") +
  theme_minimal()
```

This plot shows a steady increase in sales with seasonal fluctuations.

4.3.3 Sales by Category

Goal: Compare sales across product categories.

Code:

R

```
category_data <- data.frame(
  category = c("Electronics", "Clothing", "Home Goods", "Toys"),
  sales = c(25000, 18000, 22000, 15000)
)


ggplot(data = category_data, aes(x = reorder(category, -sales), y = sales, fill = category)) +
  geom_bar(stat = "identity") +
  labs(title = "Sales by Product Category",
      x = "Category",
      y = "Sales ($)") +
  theme_minimal()
```

This bar chart highlights which categories are driving revenue.

4.3.4 Regional Sales Breakdown

Goal: Show regional contributions to total sales.

Code:

R

```r
region_data <- data.frame(
  region = c("North", "South", "East", "West"),
  sales = c(30000, 25000, 28000, 27000)
)


ggplot(data = region_data, aes(x = "", y = sales, fill = region)) +
  geom_bar(stat = "identity", width = 1) +
  coord_polar("y") +
  labs(title = "Regional Sales Breakdown",
       fill = "Region") +
  theme_void()
```

A pie chart shows the percentage contribution of each region to total sales.

This chapter introduced the basics of data visualization using ggplot2, focusing on building impactful charts, adhering to storytelling principles, and exploring real-world examples. With these tools, you can translate raw data into insights that drive decision-making.

Chapter 5: Working with Time Series Data

5.1 Basics of Time Series Analysis in R

5.1.1 What is Time Series Data?

Time series data is a sequence of data points collected or recorded at successive points in time, typically at uniform intervals. Unlike other types of data, time series data is ordered, making temporal dependencies a critical aspect of analysis.

Examples of time series data include:

- Stock market prices recorded daily
- Monthly sales figures for a retail store
- Annual rainfall measurements

5.1.2 Key Components of Time Series Data

Time series data typically exhibits one or more of the following components:

1. **Trend**: A long-term increase or decrease in the data.

2. **Seasonality**: Regular patterns or cycles that repeat over specific intervals, such as weekly, monthly, or yearly.

3. **Cyclic Behavior**: Fluctuations occurring at irregular intervals due to economic cycles or other external factors.

4. **Noise**: Random variation not explained by the trend, seasonality, or cyclic behavior.

5.1.3 Why Time Series Analysis?

Time series analysis helps in:

- Identifying patterns in data over time.

- Making forecasts for future points based on past behavior.

- Detecting anomalies, such as unusual spikes or dips.

5.1.4 Preparing Time Series Data in R

To work with time series data in R, ensure the data is properly formatted:

- A Date or Time column is essential.

- The data should be in chronological order.

- Missing timestamps should be handled appropriately.

Example dataset:

R

```
# Sample data

data <- data.frame(

  Date = seq(as.Date("2023-01-01"), as.Date("2023-12-31"), by = "month"),

  Sales = c(500, 520, 580, 600, 620, 650, 680, 700, 720, 750, 780, 800)

)
```

5.2 Visualizing Time Series with forecast and ts Packages

5.2.1 Creating Time Series Objects

The ts function in R converts data into a time series object.

Example:

R

```
# Converting sales data to a time series object

sales_ts <- ts(data$Sales, start = c(2023, 1), frequency = 12)  # Monthly data

print(sales_ts)
```

5.2.2 Plotting Basic Time Series Data

Visualizing the data is often the first step in analysis. Use the plot function to quickly view a time series:

R

```
# Plotting the time series
plot(sales_ts, main = "Monthly Sales", xlab = "Month",
ylab = "Sales", col = "blue")
```

5.2.3 Advanced Visualization with ggplot2

For more detailed visualizations, transform the data into a format compatible with ggplot2:

R

```
library(ggplot2)


# Plotting with ggplot2
ggplot(data, aes(x = Date, y = Sales)) +
  geom_line(color = "blue") +
  labs(title = "Monthly Sales Trend", x = "Month", y =
"Sales") +
  theme_minimal()
```

5.2.4 Decomposing Time Series

Decomposing time series data separates it into its trend, seasonality, and residual components. Use the decompose function:

R

```
# Decomposing the time series

decomposed <- decompose(sales_ts)

plot(decomposed)
```

5.2.5 Forecasting with the forecast Package

The forecast package simplifies forecasting. Fit a basic exponential smoothing model using the auto.arima function:

R

```
library(forecast)


# Forecasting future sales

model <- auto.arima(sales_ts)

forecasted <- forecast(model, h = 6)  # Forecast for next 6 months

plot(forecasted)
```

5.3 Case Study: Forecasting Stock Prices

5.3.1 Dataset Overview

For this case study, we will use historical stock prices from a CSV file:

R

```
# Load the dataset
stocks <- read.csv("stock_prices.csv")
head(stocks)
```

The dataset contains columns such as:

- **Date**: The trading date.
- **Close**: The closing price of the stock.

5.3.2 Data Preprocessing

1. Convert the Date column to a Date object:

R

```
stocks$Date <- as.Date(stocks$Date, format = "%Y-%m-%d")
```

2. Sort the data by date:

R

```
stocks <- stocks[order(stocks$Date), ]
```

3. Create a time series object:

R

```r
stock_ts <- ts(stocks$Close, start = c(2010, 1),
frequency = 252)  # 252 trading days in a year
```

5.3.3 Visualizing Stock Prices

Plot the closing prices:

R

```r
ggplot(stocks, aes(x = Date, y = Close)) +
  geom_line(color = "darkgreen") +
  labs(title = "Stock Price Trend", x = "Date", y = "Closing Price") +
  theme_minimal()
```

5.3.4 Trend and Seasonality Analysis

Decompose the time series to analyze components:

R

```r
decomposed <- decompose(stock_ts)
plot(decomposed)
```

5.3.5 Building a Forecasting Model

Using ARIMA (AutoRegressive Integrated Moving Average):

R

```r
# Fit ARIMA model
```

```
library(forecast)

model <- auto.arima(stock_ts)


# Forecast future prices

forecasted_prices <- forecast(model, h = 30)  #
Forecast for the next 30 trading days

plot(forecasted_prices)
```

5.3.6 Evaluating Model Performance

Use metrics like Mean Absolute Error (MAE) or Root
Mean Square Error (RMSE) to evaluate model
accuracy:

R

```
# Calculate residuals

residuals <- residuals(model)


# Evaluate accuracy

accuracy(model)
```

5.3.7 Insights and Recommendations

Analyze the forecast and offer actionable insights:

- Identify periods of significant growth or decline.
- Use forecasts to make informed investment
  decisions.

In this chapter, we explored the fundamentals of time series analysis, from creating and visualizing time series data to decomposing and forecasting it. Using tools like ts and forecast, we developed a hands-on understanding of analyzing time-dependent data. The stock price forecasting case study demonstrated the real-world application of these techniques, highlighting the power of R for time series analysis.

Chapter 6: Introduction to Machine Learning

6.1 Machine Learning Versus Traditional Programming

Machine learning (ML) is a transformative approach to solving problems that traditional programming cannot easily address. To understand its significance, let's contrast the two paradigms.

6.1.1 Traditional Programming

In traditional programming, humans define explicit rules for the computer to follow. This requires:

- Clear problem definitions.
- Predefined algorithms.
- Explicitly coded instructions.

For instance, if you wanted to create a program to identify spam emails, you'd write rules such as:

- If the email contains certain keywords like "win money" or "free offer," mark it as spam.

- If the sender's address is in a blacklist, mark it as spam.

This approach becomes challenging as the complexity and variety of data increase. Writing and maintaining rules for every possible spam indicator is infeasible when dealing with millions of emails from diverse sources.

6.1.2 Machine Learning

Machine learning shifts the paradigm. Instead of explicitly coding rules, you provide a machine learning model with:

1. **Data**: A set of input examples (e.g., emails labeled as "spam" or "not spam").

2. **Algorithms**: The mathematical framework that allows the model to learn patterns from the data.

The model identifies the underlying patterns and creates rules on its own. In the case of spam detection, it might learn to recognize subtle indicators, such as the frequency of certain words or unusual sender domains, without human intervention.

6.1.3 Why Machine Learning is Powerful

1. **Adaptability**: Models can adjust to new patterns in the data.

2. **Scalability**: ML handles large datasets effectively.

3. **Generality**: It can solve problems across diverse fields, from predicting stock prices to diagnosing diseases.

However, machine learning also has limitations:

- Requires significant data and computational resources.

- Models can be opaque, leading to challenges in interpretation and trust.

6.2 Types of Machine Learning

Machine learning encompasses several approaches, each suited to specific types of problems. The primary types are **supervised learning**, **unsupervised learning**, and **reinforcement learning**.

6.2.1 Supervised Learning

In supervised learning, the model is trained on labeled data—datasets where the desired output (target variable) is known.

- **Goal**: Predict an outcome or classify data into predefined categories.

- **Example Problems**:

    ○ Predicting house prices based on features like size, location, and number of rooms.

- Classifying emails as "spam" or "not spam."

- **Common Algorithms**:

  - Regression (e.g., linear regression, logistic regression).

  - Decision trees and random forests.

  - Support vector machines (SVM).

  - Neural networks.

6.2.2 Unsupervised Learning

In unsupervised learning, the model works with unlabeled data. Its goal is to identify patterns, groupings, or structures in the data.

- **Goal**: Discover hidden structures or relationships in the data.

- **Example Problems**:

  - Grouping customers based on purchasing behavior (customer segmentation).

  - Detecting anomalies in network traffic (outlier detection).

- **Common Algorithms**:

  - Clustering (e.g., k-means, hierarchical clustering).

  - Dimensionality reduction (e.g., PCA, t-SNE).

6.2.3 Reinforcement Learning

Reinforcement learning involves teaching an agent to make decisions by rewarding desired behaviors and penalizing undesirable ones.

- **Goal**: Learn optimal actions in an environment to maximize cumulative rewards.

- **Example Problems**:

    o Training a robot to navigate a maze.

    o Teaching an AI agent to play games like chess or Go.

- **Core Components**:

    o **Agent**: The decision-maker.

    o **Environment**: The system in which the agent operates.

    o **Rewards**: Feedback for actions taken.

Reinforcement learning is widely used in robotics, autonomous vehicles, and game AI.

6.3 Real-World Example: Classifying Emails as Spam or Not

Let's explore a practical application of supervised learning: building a spam classifier.

6.3.1 Problem Definition

The goal is to classify incoming emails as either "spam" or "not spam." This is a binary classification problem because there are only two possible outcomes.

6.3.2 Data Collection

A labeled dataset of emails is required, where each email is paired with a label:

- **1 (spam)**: Emails flagged as unwanted or irrelevant.

- **0 (not spam)**: Emails deemed important or genuine.

Datasets like the Enron Email Dataset or synthetic datasets from online sources can be used for training.

6.3.3 Data Preprocessing

To prepare the data for machine learning, the following steps are necessary:

1. **Text Cleaning**: Remove unnecessary characters, punctuation, and stop words.

2. **Tokenization**: Break text into individual words or tokens.

3. **Feature Engineering**:

   - Count word frequencies (e.g., how often words like "free" or "money" appear).

   - Use techniques like Term Frequency-Inverse Document Frequency (TF-IDF) to weigh word importance.

4. **Splitting Data**:

   o Divide the dataset into training (70-80%) and testing (20-30%) subsets.

6.3.4 Model Building

Choose a supervised learning algorithm to train the model. A common choice for spam classification is **logistic regression** due to its simplicity and interpretability.

R


```
# Example: Logistic Regression for Spam Classification in R

library(caret)


# Load dataset (assuming it's already preprocessed)

data <- read.csv("spam_dataset.csv")


# Split into training and testing sets

set.seed(123)

trainIndex <- createDataPartition(data$label, p = 0.8, list = FALSE)

trainData <- data[trainIndex,]

testData <- data[-trainIndex,]
```

```
# Train a logistic regression model
```

```
model <- glm(label ~ ., data = trainData, family = "binomial")
```

```
# Predict on test data
```

```
predictions <- predict(model, testData, type = "response")
```

```
predicted_labels <- ifelse(predictions > 0.5, 1, 0)
```

6.3.5 Model Evaluation

Evaluate the model's performance using metrics such as:

- **Accuracy**: Proportion of correctly classified emails.

- **Precision**: Proportion of predicted spam emails that are actually spam.

- **Recall**: Proportion of actual spam emails that were correctly identified.

- **F1 Score**: Harmonic mean of precision and recall.

R

```
# Confusion matrix
```

```
conf_matrix <- confusionMatrix(as.factor(predicted_labels), as.factor(testData$label))
```

```
print(conf_matrix)
```

6.3.6 Deployment

After training and validating the model, integrate it into an email filtering system. Use R's Plumber package or deploy the model on cloud platforms to process incoming emails in real time.

6.3.7 Challenges

1. **False Positives**: Legitimate emails incorrectly flagged as spam.

2. **Evolving Nature of Spam**: Spammers adapt, requiring continuous model updates.

3. **Interpretability**: Ensuring stakeholders trust the model's decisions.

This chapter introduced the fundamentals of machine learning, contrasting it with traditional programming. We explored the main types of machine learning—supervised, unsupervised, and reinforcement learning—and applied these concepts to a real-world example: classifying emails as spam or not.

Chapter 7: Data Preprocessing for Machine Learning

7.1 The Importance of Data Preprocessing

Data preprocessing is the foundation of any successful machine learning project. Raw data is rarely ready for direct use in models; it often contains inconsistencies, missing values, or variables in incompatible formats. Preprocessing ensures the data is clean, consistent, and suitable for analysis. This process involves:

- Splitting data into training and testing sets.

- Normalizing or scaling numerical features.

- Encoding categorical variables into numerical formats.

Effective preprocessing improves model accuracy, reduces bias, and speeds up training.

7.2 Splitting Data into Training and Testing Sets

When building machine learning models, it's crucial to evaluate their performance on unseen data. This is achieved by splitting the dataset into:

1. **Training Set**: Used to train the model.

2. **Testing Set**: Used to evaluate the model's performance.

The typical split ratio is 70-80% for training and 20-30% for testing, though it may vary depending on the dataset size.

7.2.1 Why Split the Data?

The goal is to assess how well the model generalizes to new data. Training and testing on the same dataset can lead to overfitting, where the model performs well on training data but poorly on unseen data.

7.2.2 Implementing a Data Split in R

The caret and dplyr packages make splitting data straightforward.

Example

Suppose we have a dataset for customer churn analysis:

R

```
library(caret)
```

```
library(dplyr)

# Example dataset
data <- read.csv("customer_data.csv")

# Splitting the data
set.seed(123)  # Ensures reproducibility
trainIndex <- createDataPartition(data$Churn, p = 0.8,
list = FALSE)
train <- data[trainIndex, ]
test <- data[-trainIndex, ]
```
Here:

- createDataPartition() ensures stratified sampling, keeping the target variable distribution consistent across training and testing sets.

- p = 0.8 splits the data with 80% for training and 20% for testing.

7.3 Normalization and Scaling

Machine learning algorithms like k-NN, SVMs, and neural networks are sensitive to feature scales. Normalization and scaling help standardize numerical features, ensuring no variable dominates due to its magnitude.

7.3.1 Normalization

Normalization rescales features to a range of [0, 1]. It is especially useful when the data contains features with varying units or ranges.

Formula for Normalization

x'=x−min(x)max(x)−min(x)x' = \frac{x - \text{min}(x)}{\text{max}(x) - \text{min}(x)}x'=max(x)−min(x)x−min(x)

Implementation in R

R

```
normalize <- function(x) {
  return((x - min(x)) / (max(x) - min(x)))
}


# Apply normalization to selected columns
data$Income <- normalize(data$Income)
data$Age <- normalize(data$Age)
```

7.3.2 Scaling (Standardization)

Scaling transforms features to have a mean of 0 and a standard deviation of 1. This approach is preferred for algorithms sensitive to feature magnitudes, such as logistic regression or PCA.

Formula for Scaling

$z = \frac{x - \mu}{\sigma}$

Where μ is the mean, and σ is the standard deviation.

Implementation in R

R

```
# Standardize numerical columns

data$Income <- scale(data$Income)

data$Age <- scale(data$Age)
```

7.3.3 Which to Use?

- Use **normalization** when features are non-Gaussian or bounded (e.g., pixel intensities).

- Use **scaling** when data follows a normal distribution or when applying algorithms like SVM or PCA.

7.4 Encoding Categorical Variables

Machine learning models work with numerical data, so categorical variables must be converted into a numerical format. R offers several approaches for encoding:

7.4.1 Label Encoding

Each category is assigned a unique integer. This approach is simple but may introduce ordinal relationships that don't exist.

Example

R

```r
data$Gender <- as.numeric(factor(data$Gender))
```

7.4.2 One-Hot Encoding

Each category is represented as a binary feature. This approach avoids introducing ordinal relationships and is widely used.

Example Using caret

R

```r
library(caret)

# One-hot encoding
dummyVars <- dummyVars(~ Gender + Region, data = data)
encodedData <- predict(dummyVars, newdata = data)
data <- cbind(data, encodedData)
```

7.4.3 Encoding for High-Cardinality Features

For features with many unique categories (e.g., ZIP codes or product IDs), encoding can lead to a high-dimensional dataset. Techniques like target encoding or embeddings (in deep learning) may be more efficient.

7.5 Example: Preparing Data for Predicting Customer Churn

7.5.1 Problem Definition

A telecommunications company wants to predict customer churn based on features like demographics, usage patterns, and contract details. The dataset includes:

- **Numerical features**: MonthlyCharges, Tenure, TotalCharges.

- **Categorical features**: Gender, PaymentMethod, ContractType.

- **Target variable**: Churn (Yes/No).

7.5.2 Data Preprocessing Steps

Step 1: Load and Inspect the Data

R

```r
data <- read.csv("telco_customer_churn.csv")
str(data)
summary(data)
```

Key tasks:

- Check for missing values.

- Identify data types (numerical or categorical).

Step 2: Handle Missing Values

R

```r
# Replace missing values in TotalCharges with the median
data$TotalCharges[is.na(data$TotalCharges)] <-
median(data$TotalCharges, na.rm = TRUE)
```

Step 3: Encode Categorical Variables

R

```r
# Convert categorical variables to factors
data$Gender <- as.factor(data$Gender)
data$PaymentMethod <-
as.factor(data$PaymentMethod)


# One-hot encoding
```

```r
dummyVars <- dummyVars(~ PaymentMethod +
ContractType, data = data)

encoded <- predict(dummyVars, newdata = data)

data <- cbind(data, encoded)
```

Step 4: Normalize Numerical Features

R

```r
# Normalize numerical columns

data$MonthlyCharges <-
normalize(data$MonthlyCharges)

data$Tenure <- normalize(data$Tenure)

data$TotalCharges <- normalize(data$TotalCharges)
```

Step 5: Split the Data

R

```r
set.seed(42)

trainIndex <- createDataPartition(data$Churn, p = 0.8,
list = FALSE)

train <- data[trainIndex, ]

test <- data[-trainIndex, ]
```

7.5.3 Ready for Modeling

After preprocessing, the dataset is clean and
structured for machine learning. You can now train a

logistic regression model or a random forest to predict customer churn.

In this chapter, we covered the essential steps for preprocessing data for machine learning:

1. Splitting data into training and testing sets to prevent overfitting.

2. Normalizing and scaling numerical variables for consistency.

3. Encoding categorical variables for compatibility with machine learning algorithms.

The example of preparing a customer churn dataset demonstrated these techniques in action. These preprocessing steps are critical for building robust machine learning models. In the next chapter, we'll explore linear regression and its practical applications.

Chapter 8: Linear Regression

Linear regression is a cornerstone of data analysis and machine learning, offering a straightforward yet powerful way to model relationships between variables. In this chapter, we'll explore both simple and multiple linear regression in R, breaking down the concepts with clear explanations and guiding you through a real-world example: predicting housing prices.

8.1 What is Linear Regression?

Linear regression is a statistical method used to model the relationship between one or more independent variables (predictors) and a dependent variable (outcome). The goal is to find the best-fitting line (or plane in the case of multiple predictors) that minimizes the difference between observed and predicted values.

8.1.1 Key Concepts of Linear Regression

- **Dependent Variable (Y)**: The variable we want to predict.

- **Independent Variable(s) (X)**: The variable(s) we use to make predictions.

- **Line Equation**: $Y = \beta_0 + \beta_1 X + \epsilon$, where:

  - β_0: Intercept of the regression line.

  - β_1: Slope of the regression line, representing the change in Y for a one-unit change in X.

  - ϵ: Error term, accounting for deviations of the actual data points from the predicted line.

8.1.2 Types of Linear Regression

- **Simple Linear Regression**: Models the relationship between one independent variable and one dependent variable.

- **Multiple Linear Regression**: Extends simple linear regression to include two or more independent variables.

8.2 Simple Linear Regression in R

8.2.1 The Concept

Simple linear regression predicts a dependent variable based on a single independent variable. For example, predicting house prices based solely on square footage.

8.2.2 Example: Predicting Housing Prices

Let's start with a dataset containing information on housing prices and their square footage.

Step 1: Load the Data

R

```
# Simulate housing data
housing_data <- data.frame(
  square_footage = c(1000, 1500, 2000, 2500, 3000),
  price = c(200000, 250000, 300000, 350000, 400000)
)
```

Step 2: Visualize the Data

Visualizing the data can help us understand the relationship between the variables.

R

```
library(ggplot2)

ggplot(housing_data, aes(x = square_footage, y = price)) +
```

```
geom_point() +

labs(title = "Housing Prices vs. Square Footage",

    x = "Square Footage",

    y = "Price")
```

Step 3: Fit the Model

Use the lm() function to fit a simple linear regression model.

R

```
# Fit the model

model <- lm(price ~ square_footage, data =
housing_data)


# View the model summary

summary(model)
```

8.2.3 Interpreting the Results

- **Coefficients**: The model outputs an intercept and a slope. For example:
    - Intercept (β_0\beta_0$\beta0$): $100,000
    - Slope (β_1\beta_1$\beta1$): $100 per square foot
- **Interpretation**: For every additional square foot, the price increases by $100.

Step 4: Make Predictions

R

```r
# Predict prices for new square footage values
new_data <- data.frame(square_footage = c(1200, 1800, 2400))
predictions <- predict(model, newdata = new_data)
predictions
```

Step 5: Plot the Regression Line

R

```r
# Add the regression line to the plot
ggplot(housing_data, aes(x = square_footage, y = price)) +
  geom_point() +
  geom_smooth(method = "lm", se = FALSE, color = "blue") +
  labs(title = "Simple Linear Regression: Housing Prices",
       x = "Square Footage",
       y = "Price")
```

8.3 Multiple Linear Regression in R

8.3.1 The Concept

Multiple linear regression involves more than one predictor variable. For instance, housing prices may depend not only on square footage but also on the number of bedrooms, location, and age of the house.

8.3.2 Example: Predicting Housing Prices with Multiple Predictors

Let's extend our dataset to include additional predictors.

Step 1: Load the Data

R

```
# Simulate housing data
housing_data <- data.frame(
  square_footage = c(1000, 1500, 2000, 2500, 3000),
  bedrooms = c(2, 3, 3, 4, 4),
  age = c(10, 15, 20, 25, 30),
  price = c(200000, 250000, 300000, 350000, 400000)
)
```

Step 2: Fit the Model

R

```
# Fit the multiple regression model

multi_model <- lm(price ~ square_footage +
bedrooms + age, data = housing_data)


# View the model summary

summary(multi_model)
```

8.3.3 Interpreting the Results

- **Coefficients**: The output includes coefficients for each predictor variable:
    - Square Footage: For every additional square foot, the price increases by $100.
    - Bedrooms: Each additional bedroom adds $20,000 to the price.
    - Age: Each additional year decreases the price by $1,000.
- **Statistical Significance**: Check the p-values to determine which predictors significantly influence the dependent variable.

Step 3: Make Predictions

R


```
# Predict prices for new data

new_data <- data.frame(

  square_footage = c(1200, 1800, 2400),
```

```
  bedrooms = c(3, 3, 4),

  age = c(10, 15, 20)

)
```

```
predictions <- predict(multi_model, newdata = new_data)
```

```
predictions
```

Step 4: Visualize Model Fit

Since visualizing multiple predictors is challenging, focus on key relationships using partial plots or correlation heatmaps.

8.4 Model Diagnostics

Before trusting the regression model, it's essential to evaluate its assumptions:

1. **Linearity**: The relationship between predictors and the outcome is linear.

2. **Normality**: Residuals (errors) should be normally distributed.

3. **Homoscedasticity**: Residuals should have constant variance.

4. **Multicollinearity**: Predictors should not be too highly correlated.

Diagnostic Tools in R

R

```
# Residual plots

plot(multi_model)


# Check for multicollinearity

library(car)

vif(multi_model)  # Variance Inflation Factor (VIF)
```

8.5 Real-World Example: Predicting Housing Prices

The Scenario

A real estate company wants to predict house prices based on features such as square footage, number of bedrooms, and the house's age. Using historical data, you will develop a regression model to assist with pricing decisions.

Step-by-Step Approach

1. **Data Collection**: Gather historical data from real estate records or online platforms.

2. **Exploratory Data Analysis (EDA)**:

    o Use summary() and str() to understand the dataset.

- Create scatterplots to visualize relationships between predictors and the target variable.

3. **Feature Engineering**: Create new features if needed (e.g., price per square foot).

4. **Model Building**: Use multiple linear regression to develop the model.

5. **Model Validation**:

   - Split the data into training and testing sets.

   - Evaluate the model's performance using metrics like R-squared, RMSE, and MAE.

Linear regression is a powerful and interpretable tool for predictive modeling. In this chapter, you learned to:

1. Understand the fundamentals of simple and multiple linear regression.

2. Apply these concepts in R using the lm() function.

3. Diagnose model assumptions and validate predictions.

4. Build a real-world regression model to predict housing prices.

Chapter 9: Classification with Logistic Regression

9.1 Logistic Regression and Its Real-World Applications

Logistic regression is a foundational machine learning algorithm widely used for classification problems. Unlike linear regression, which predicts continuous values, logistic regression predicts categorical outcomes. This makes it especially useful in scenarios where the goal is to classify data into distinct categories.

9.1.1 What is Logistic Regression?

Logistic regression models the probability that a given input belongs to a specific category. It is particularly suited for binary classification, where the target variable has only two possible outcomes, such as:

- Spam vs. Not Spam

- Churn vs. Retained

- Pass vs. Fail

The logistic regression algorithm calculates the probability of an event occurring using the logistic function (also known as the sigmoid function):

$$P(Y=1|X) = \frac{1}{1 + e^{-(\beta_0 + \beta_1 X_1 + \beta_2 X_2 + ... + \beta_n X_n)}}$$

Here:

- $P(Y=1|X)$ is the probability of the target being in class 1.

- β_0 is the intercept.

- $\beta_1, \beta_2, ..., \beta_n$ are coefficients corresponding to input features.

The result is a probability value between 0 and 1. A threshold (e.g., 0.5) is then applied to classify the output into categories.

9.1.2 Real-World Applications of Logistic Regression

Logistic regression is popular because it is interpretable, efficient, and works well on relatively simple datasets. Some practical applications include:

1. **Employee Attrition Prediction**
   Companies use logistic regression to identify employees likely to leave, helping them take proactive retention measures.

2. **Fraud Detection**
   Credit card providers analyze transaction patterns to classify transactions as fraudulent or legitimate.

3. **Medical Diagnostics**
   Logistic regression helps predict the presence or absence of diseases based on patient symptoms and test results.

4. **Customer Churn Prediction**
   Businesses analyze customer behavior to classify whether a customer will churn or remain loyal.

5. **Credit Approval**
   Logistic regression evaluates loan applications by predicting whether an applicant is likely to repay based on financial and demographic factors.

9.2 Hands-On Example: Predicting Employee Attrition

Let's walk through a practical example of using logistic regression to predict employee attrition. Imagine you are an HR analyst tasked with identifying employees who are likely to leave their jobs based on factors like satisfaction level, salary, and work hours.

9.2.1 Step 1: Understand the Problem

The goal is to predict whether an employee will leave (attrition = 1) or stay (attrition = 0) using features such as:

- **Satisfaction Level**: Employee's satisfaction score (0–1).

- **Last Evaluation**: Score of the last performance review.

- **Average Monthly Hours**: Average hours worked per month.

- **Number of Projects**: Number of projects the employee is handling.

9.2.2 Step 2: Load and Inspect the Data

Load the dataset into R and inspect it. For this example, we'll use a sample dataset named employee_attrition.csv.

R

```
# Load necessary libraries
library(tidyverse)


# Load the dataset
attrition_data <- read.csv("employee_attrition.csv")


# Inspect the data
```

```
head(attrition_data)
```

```
summary(attrition_data)
```

The dataset might look like this:

Satisfaction_Level	Last_Evaluation	Avg_Monthly_Hours	Num_Projects	Attrition
0.75	0.85	220	4	0
0.62	0.70	250	5	1

9.2.3 Step 3: Exploratory Data Analysis (EDA)

Before building the model, it's essential to explore the data:

1. Check for missing values.
2. Understand the distributions of features.
3. Visualize relationships between features and the target variable.

R

```
# Check for missing values

colSums(is.na(attrition_data))


# Visualize Satisfaction Level vs. Attrition

ggplot(attrition_data, aes(x = Satisfaction_Level, fill =
factor(Attrition))) +
```

```
geom_histogram(position = "dodge", bins = 20) +

labs(title = "Satisfaction Level and Attrition", fill =
"Attrition")
```

9.2.4 Step 4: Preprocess the Data

Prepare the data for modeling:

- Convert categorical variables to factors.
- Split the data into training and testing sets.

R

```
# Convert Attrition to a factor

attrition_data$Attrition <-
as.factor(attrition_data$Attrition)


# Split into training and testing sets

set.seed(123)

train_index <- sample(1:nrow(attrition_data), 0.7 *
nrow(attrition_data))

train_data <- attrition_data[train_index, ]

test_data <- attrition_data[-train_index, ]
```

9.2.5 Step 5: Build the Logistic Regression Model

Fit a logistic regression model using the glm() function.

R

```
# Build the logistic regression model

attrition_model <- glm(Attrition ~ Satisfaction_Level +
Last_Evaluation + Avg_Monthly_Hours +
Num_Projects,

                data = train_data, family = binomial)


# Summarize the model

summary(attrition_model)
```

9.2.6 Step 6: Evaluate the Model

Assess the model's performance using accuracy, precision, recall, and the confusion matrix.

R

```
# Make predictions

predicted_probs <- predict(attrition_model, test_data,
type = "response")

predicted_classes <- ifelse(predicted_probs > 0.5, 1,
0)
```

```
# Confusion matrix

table(Predicted = predicted_classes, Actual =
test_data$Attrition)


# Calculate accuracy

accuracy <- mean(predicted_classes ==
test_data$Attrition)

print(paste("Accuracy:", accuracy))
```

9.2.7 Step 7: Interpret the Results

Interpret the coefficients from the model:

- Positive coefficients indicate that as the variable increases, the likelihood of attrition also increases.
- Negative coefficients suggest the opposite.

For instance:

- A negative coefficient for **Satisfaction_Level** suggests that higher satisfaction levels reduce the likelihood of attrition.

9.2.8 Step 8: Use the Model for Predictions

Once satisfied with the model, use it to predict attrition for new employees.

R

```
# Example: Predict for a new employee

new_employee <- data.frame(Satisfaction_Level =
0.6, Last_Evaluation = 0.75,

                  Avg_Monthly_Hours = 200,
Num_Projects = 3)


predicted_prob <- predict(attrition_model,
new_employee, type = "response")

predicted_class <- ifelse(predicted_prob > 0.5, 1, 0)


print(paste("Predicted Attrition:", predicted_class))
```

In this chapter, we explored logistic regression, one of
the most accessible and interpretable classification
models. By walking through a real-world example of
predicting employee attrition, we saw how logistic
regression can be applied from start to finish,
including:

1. Understanding the problem and preparing the
   data.

2. Building and interpreting a logistic regression
   model.

3. Evaluating its performance and using it for
   predictions.

Logistic regression remains a powerful tool for solving binary classification problems, especially when explainability and simplicity are critical. In the next chapter, we'll delve into tree-based models, which offer an alternative approach to classification problems with higher flexibility and power.

Chapter 10: Tree-Based Models

10.1 Introduction to Tree-Based Models

Tree-based models are a class of predictive algorithms used for both regression and classification tasks. These models structure data into decision trees, resembling a flowchart, where each split represents a decision rule, and the leaves represent outcomes. The beauty of tree-based models lies in their interpretability and flexibility.

What Makes Tree-Based Models Valuable?

- **Interpretability**: They provide a clear path of decisions leading to a prediction.

- **Non-linearity**: Tree models can capture complex relationships in data.

- **Versatility**: Suitable for classification and regression tasks across various industries.

- **Minimal Preprocessing**: They handle categorical and numerical data naturally, requiring less data preprocessing.

In this chapter, we explore three key tree-based models: **decision trees, random forests**, and **gradient boosting**, focusing on their applications in real-world customer segmentation.

10.2 Decision Trees

A **decision tree** is a tree-like structure where each node represents a feature, each branch represents a decision rule, and each leaf node represents an outcome. It splits the dataset into smaller subsets by asking a series of binary questions.

10.2.1 How Decision Trees Work

1. **Split Selection**: At each node, the algorithm chooses the feature and threshold that best split the data based on a criterion (e.g., Gini impurity, entropy for classification, or mean squared error for regression).

2. **Recursive Splitting**: The process repeats for each subset until a stopping criterion is met (e.g., a maximum depth or minimum number of samples per leaf).

3. **Prediction**: For classification, the outcome is the majority class in the leaf; for regression, it's the mean of the target variable.

10.2.2 Advantages and Limitations

Advantages:

- Easy to understand and visualize.
- Handles both categorical and numerical data.
- Captures interactions between variables.

Limitations:

- Prone to overfitting, especially with deep trees.
- Sensitive to small changes in data, leading to instability.

10.2.3 Example: Using Decision Trees for Customer Segmentation

Suppose we want to segment customers of a retail store into groups based on their purchasing behavior. Here's how we could approach it:

1. **Data**: Customer attributes (e.g., age, income, frequency of purchases, average spending).

2. **Objective**: Classify customers into "High-Value," "Medium-Value," and "Low-Value" groups.

3. **Steps**:
   - Split the dataset into training and testing sets.
   - Train a decision tree classifier using the rpart package in R.
   - Evaluate the model using accuracy and visualizations.

10.3 Random Forests

A **random forest** is an ensemble method that builds multiple decision trees and combines their outputs to improve accuracy and reduce overfitting.

10.3.1 How Random Forests Work

1. **Bootstrap Sampling**: Randomly sample the dataset with replacement to create multiple subsets.

2. **Tree Construction**: Build a decision tree for each subset, but at each split, randomly select a subset of features to consider.

3. **Aggregation**: Combine the predictions of all trees:

   o For classification, use majority voting.

   o For regression, calculate the average prediction.

10.3.2 Why Use Random Forests?

- **Reduced Overfitting**: The ensemble approach generalizes better than individual trees.

- **Robustness**: It's less sensitive to noise in the data.

- **Feature Importance**: Random forests can rank the importance of features based on their contribution to predictions.

10.3.3 Example: Customer Segmentation with Random Forests

Continuing our retail store example:

1. Train a random forest classifier using the randomForest package in R.

2. Interpret the feature importance to understand which attributes (e.g., income, frequency) are most predictive.

3. Evaluate performance using cross-validation and confusion matrices.

Random forests not only improve prediction accuracy but also provide insights into the key factors influencing customer behavior.

10.4 Gradient Boosting

Gradient boosting is another ensemble method that builds trees sequentially, with each tree attempting to correct the errors of the previous ones. Unlike random forests, which aggregate independent trees, gradient boosting focuses on incremental learning.

10.4.1 How Gradient Boosting Works

1. **Initialize the Model**: Start with a simple prediction (e.g., the mean value of the target).

2. **Iterative Training**:

   o Fit a tree to the residual errors of the current model.

- Update the model by adding the new tree to minimize the loss function.

3. **Combine Models**: Repeat the process until a stopping criterion is met (e.g., number of trees or convergence).

10.4.2 Popular Implementations in R

- **xgboost**: Known for its speed and performance.

- **gbm**: A robust implementation of gradient boosting.

- **catboost**: Optimized for categorical data.

10.4.3 Advantages and Limitations

Advantages:

- Handles imbalanced datasets effectively.

- High accuracy for complex datasets.

- Customizable loss functions.

Limitations:

- Computationally intensive.

- Prone to overfitting without careful tuning.

10.4.4 Example: Gradient Boosting for Customer Segmentation

Using the same dataset:

1. Train a gradient boosting model with the xgboost package.

2. Tune hyperparameters (e.g., learning rate, number of trees) using grid search or cross-validation.

3. Evaluate the model using metrics like F1-score, precision, and recall.

The sequential learning approach of gradient boosting often outperforms random forests when tuned correctly.

10.5 Case Study: Customer Segmentation

Problem Statement:
A retail business wants to classify customers into segments to design targeted marketing campaigns.

Dataset:

- **Features**: Age, income, purchase frequency, average transaction amount, customer tenure.

- **Target**: Customer segments (High-Value, Medium-Value, Low-Value).

Steps to Solve the Problem

1. **Exploratory Data Analysis (EDA)**:

   o Visualize feature distributions.

- o Identify correlations between features and the target.

2. **Feature Engineering**:
   - o Create derived features (e.g., annual spending).
   - o Encode categorical variables.

3. **Modeling**:
   - o Train a decision tree to understand the segmentation rules.
   - o Use a random forest to improve accuracy.
   - o Experiment with gradient boosting for fine-tuned results.

4. **Evaluation**:
   - o Compare models using metrics like accuracy, precision, recall, and AUC-ROC.
   - o Interpret feature importance to provide actionable insights.

5. **Actionable Insights**:
   - o High-value customers: Design loyalty programs.
   - o Medium-value customers: Offer incentives to increase spending.
   - o Low-value customers: Focus on retention strategies.

Tree-based models are indispensable tools in data science, providing a balance of interpretability and power. Decision trees offer simplicity and transparency, random forests enhance stability and accuracy, and gradient boosting delivers cutting-edge performance. By applying these models to customer segmentation, businesses can unlock valuable insights, enabling data-driven decisions that foster growth and customer satisfaction.

Chapter 11: Clustering and Unsupervised Learning

11.1 Introduction to Clustering and Unsupervised Learning

Clustering is one of the most popular techniques in **unsupervised learning**, where the goal is to find patterns and groupings in data without predefined labels or categories. Unlike supervised learning, which works with labeled datasets, clustering algorithms infer structure by identifying similarities or relationships between data points.

11.1.1 What is Clustering?

Clustering involves grouping data points into clusters such that points within the same cluster are more similar to each other than to those in other clusters. Here's a practical example:

- A retailer might use clustering to segment customers into groups based on their purchasing behavior, which helps target marketing efforts.

11.1.2 Applications of Clustering

Clustering has broad applications across industries:

- **Marketing**: Customer segmentation for targeted campaigns.

- **Healthcare**: Grouping patients based on medical conditions or responses to treatments.

- **Social Networks**: Detecting communities or groups of friends.

- **Document Classification**: Organizing articles or research papers into thematic categories.

- **Retail**: Identifying buying patterns or recommending products.

11.1.3 Types of Clustering Algorithms

1. **Partitioning Algorithms**: These create non-overlapping clusters of data points.

   - Example: k-means clustering.

2. **Hierarchical Algorithms**: These build a tree of clusters (dendrogram) that shows how clusters merge or split.

   - Example: hierarchical clustering.

3. **Density-Based Clustering**: Groups data points based on density; useful for detecting arbitrarily shaped clusters.

   - Example: DBSCAN.

11.2 Introduction to k-Means Clustering

k-means is one of the simplest and most commonly used clustering algorithms. It aims to partition data into k clusters, where each cluster is defined by its centroid (center point).

11.2.1 How k-Means Works

1. **Select k (number of clusters)**: You must specify the desired number of clusters.

2. **Initialize Centroids**: Randomly select k points as initial cluster centers.

3. **Assign Points to Clusters**: Each data point is assigned to the cluster whose centroid is closest, typically using the Euclidean distance.

4. **Update Centroids**: Compute the new centroid as the mean of all points in a cluster.

5. **Repeat**: Steps 3 and 4 are repeated until centroids no longer change significantly (convergence).

11.2.2 Choosing k: The Elbow Method

Choosing the right number of clusters is critical for meaningful results. One way to determine k is by using the elbow method:

- Plot the total within-cluster sum of squares (WCSS) against the number of clusters.

- The "elbow point," where the rate of decrease slows, suggests an optimal k.

11.2.3 Implementing k-Means in R

Here's a step-by-step example of k-means clustering in R:

R

```
# Load necessary library
library(ggplot2)

# Create sample data
set.seed(123)
data <- data.frame(
  x = rnorm(100, mean = 5, sd = 2),
  y = rnorm(100, mean = 3, sd = 1)
)

# Apply k-means clustering
kmeans_result <- kmeans(data, centers = 3)

# Add cluster assignment to data
data$cluster <- as.factor(kmeans_result$cluster)
```

```
# Visualize the clusters

ggplot(data, aes(x = x, y = y, color = cluster)) +

 geom_point(size = 3) +

 labs(title = "k-Means Clustering", x = "X-Axis", y =
"Y-Axis")
```

11.3 Introduction to Hierarchical Clustering

Hierarchical clustering builds a hierarchy of clusters in either an **agglomerative** (bottom-up) or **divisive** (top-down) manner.

11.3.1 Agglomerative Clustering

Agglomerative clustering begins with each data point as its own cluster and iteratively merges clusters based on similarity until a single cluster remains.

11.3.2 Divisive Clustering

Divisive clustering starts with all data points in one cluster and iteratively splits them into smaller clusters.

11.3.3 Linkage Criteria

The way clusters are merged or split depends on the linkage criterion:

- **Single Linkage**: Minimum distance between points in clusters.

- **Complete Linkage**: Maximum distance between points in clusters.

- **Average Linkage**: Average distance between all pairs of points.

11.3.4 Dendrograms

A dendrogram is a tree diagram that visualizes the merging process in hierarchical clustering. You can "cut" the dendrogram at different heights to define clusters.

11.3.5 Implementing Hierarchical Clustering in R

Here's how to perform hierarchical clustering in R:

R

```
# Generate sample data
set.seed(456)
data <- matrix(rnorm(50), nrow = 10, ncol = 5)


# Compute distance matrix
dist_matrix <- dist(data)


# Perform hierarchical clustering
hclust_result <- hclust(dist_matrix, method = "complete")
```

```
# Plot dendrogram

plot(hclust_result, main = "Dendrogram", xlab = "",
sub = "")
```

11.4 Real-World Application: Grouping Customers by Purchasing Behavior

11.4.1 Problem Statement

Imagine you are working for an e-commerce company that wants to group customers based on their purchasing behavior. These groupings will be used for targeted marketing campaigns.

11.4.2 Dataset

The dataset contains the following fields:

- **CustomerID**: Unique identifier for each customer.

- **PurchaseFrequency**: Number of purchases made.

- **AverageSpend**: Average amount spent per purchase.

- **LastPurchaseDaysAgo**: Number of days since the last purchase.

11.4.3 Steps to Perform Clustering

1. **Data Preprocessing**:

- Normalize the data to ensure that variables with larger scales don't dominate the clustering process.
- Handle missing values and outliers.

2. **Exploratory Data Analysis**:
   - Visualize relationships between variables.
   - Identify potential groupings.

3. **Clustering**:
   - Use k-means or hierarchical clustering to segment customers.
   - Determine the optimal number of clusters using the elbow method.

4. **Interpreting Results**:
   - Analyze the characteristics of each cluster to generate actionable insights.

11.4.4 Implementation in R

R

```
# Sample dataset
customer_data <- data.frame(
  PurchaseFrequency = c(5, 20, 15, 8, 25),
  AverageSpend = c(200, 150, 300, 250, 100),
```

```r
  LastPurchaseDaysAgo = c(10, 30, 5, 20, 15)

)


# Normalize the data

scaled_data <- scale(customer_data)


# Apply k-means clustering

set.seed(789)

kmeans_result <- kmeans(scaled_data, centers = 3)


# Add cluster labels to the dataset

customer_data$Cluster <-
as.factor(kmeans_result$cluster)


# Visualize clusters

library(ggplot2)

ggplot(customer_data, aes(x = PurchaseFrequency, y
= AverageSpend, color = Cluster)) +

  geom_point(size = 3) +

  labs(title = "Customer Segmentation", x = "Purchase
Frequency", y = "Average Spend")
```

11.4.5 Insights

- **Cluster 1**: High spenders with frequent purchases.

- **Cluster 2**: Moderate spenders with infrequent purchases.

- **Cluster 3**: Low spenders who purchase sporadically.

These insights can guide personalized promotions or loyalty programs.

This chapter introduced clustering as a powerful unsupervised learning technique and explored its application through k-means and hierarchical clustering. You learned how to implement clustering in R and saw its relevance in a real-world context— segmenting customers by purchasing behavior. By leveraging clustering, businesses can unlock hidden patterns in data and create tailored strategies that resonate with their audiences

Chapter 12: Dimensionality Reduction

12.1 Introduction to Dimensionality Reduction

In data science, dimensionality reduction is the process of reducing the number of features or variables in a dataset while preserving its most important information. With the increasing size and complexity of datasets, this technique has become critical for efficient and effective data analysis.

Why is Dimensionality Reduction Important?

1. **Improves Model Performance**: Many machine learning algorithms struggle with high-dimensional data, leading to overfitting or increased computational costs.

2. **Enhances Visualization**: Data in two or three dimensions is easier to interpret and visualize compared to higher dimensions.

3. **Simplifies Data**: Reducing irrelevant or redundant features can clarify relationships and patterns.

4. **Speeds Up Computation**: Fewer features mean quicker training and prediction times for machine learning models.

Two Approaches to Dimensionality Reduction

1. **Feature Selection**: Identifying and retaining only the most relevant features, such as using statistical tests or algorithms like Recursive Feature Elimination (RFE).

2. **Feature Extraction**: Creating new features by transforming the original ones. Examples include Principal Component Analysis (PCA) and t-Distributed Stochastic Neighbor Embedding (t-SNE).

12.2 Principal Component Analysis (PCA)

PCA is one of the most widely used methods for dimensionality reduction. It transforms the original variables into a new set of orthogonal components called principal components, which capture the maximum variance in the data.

12.2.1 How PCA Works

1. **Standardize the Data**: Ensures all variables contribute equally to the analysis by scaling them to have a mean of 0 and standard deviation of 1.

2. **Compute the Covariance Matrix**: Measures how variables are related to each other.

3. **Calculate Eigenvalues and Eigenvectors**: Eigenvalues measure the variance captured by each principal component, while eigenvectors define their direction.

4. **Choose Principal Components**: Select the top components that explain the majority of the variance.

5. **Transform the Data**: Project the data onto the selected components to reduce its dimensions.

12.2.2 Visualizing PCA

PCA can reduce multidimensional data into two or three dimensions for visualization. For instance:

- A scatterplot of the first two principal components can reveal clusters or trends.

- A scree plot helps determine the number of components to retain by plotting eigenvalues against their rank.

12.2.3 Example of PCA

Let's consider a dataset with customer demographics and transaction history. PCA could help identify patterns like:

- Spending habits based on a few key dimensions.

- Clustering customers with similar behaviors.

R

```r
# Example: PCA on a customer demographics dataset
library(tidyverse)
library(ggplot2)
library(stats)

# Load data
data <- scale(customer_data)  # Standardizing data

# Perform PCA
pca_result <- prcomp(data, scale. = TRUE)

# Summary of PCA
summary(pca_result)

# Visualize the first two components
pca_data <- as.data.frame(pca_result$x)
ggplot(pca_data, aes(x = PC1, y = PC2)) +
  geom_point() +
```

```
labs(title = "PCA Visualization", x = "Principal
Component 1", y = "Principal Component 2")
```

12.3 t-Distributed Stochastic Neighbor Embedding (t-SNE)

While PCA is a linear method, t-SNE is a nonlinear dimensionality reduction technique designed for visualizing high-dimensional data in two or three dimensions.

12.3.1 How t-SNE Works

1. **Calculate Pairwise Similarities**: Measures the probability that two points are neighbors in high-dimensional space.

2. **Map to Low-Dimensional Space**: Creates a similar distribution in a lower dimension while preserving local relationships.

3. **Optimize**: Minimizes the divergence between the high-dimensional and low-dimensional distributions using an iterative approach.

12.3.2 Key Features of t-SNE

- **Focuses on Local Structures**: Captures clusters or groups well but may not preserve global structures.

- **Parameter Sensitivity**: Parameters like perplexity and learning rate significantly affect results.

12.3.3 Example of t-SNE

Suppose we have an e-commerce dataset with thousands of products and their attributes. t-SNE can help:

- Cluster products based on attributes such as price, category, and customer reviews.

- Identify relationships between similar products.

R

```
# Example: t-SNE on product data
library(Rtsne)
library(ggplot2)


# Prepare data
product_data <- scale(product_dataset) #
Standardizing


# Perform t-SNE
tsne_result <- Rtsne(product_data, dims = 2,
perplexity = 30, verbose = TRUE, max_iter = 500)


# Visualize the results
tsne_data <- as.data.frame(tsne_result$Y)
ggplot(tsne_data, aes(x = V1, y = V2)) +
```

geom_point() +

labs(title = "t-SNE Visualization", x = "Dimension 1", y = "Dimension 2")

12.4 Case Study: Reducing Features in a Large E-Commerce Dataset

Imagine you are working with an e-commerce company that has a dataset containing the following attributes for each product:

- **Categorical Attributes**: Category, brand, color.

- **Numerical Attributes**: Price, ratings, sales figures.

- **Textual Attributes**: Customer reviews.

This dataset has over 500 features, making it challenging to analyze or model effectively. Dimensionality reduction helps simplify the dataset without losing valuable insights.

Step 1: Preprocessing

1. Handle missing values using imputation techniques.

2. Convert categorical variables into numerical representations (e.g., one-hot encoding).

3. Standardize numerical features.

Step 2: Apply PCA

1. Use PCA to identify components explaining at least 95% of the variance.

2. Reduce the dataset to these principal components.

Step 3: Apply t-SNE

1. Apply t-SNE to visualize product clusters based on selected components.

2. Identify patterns, such as which clusters correspond to high sales or customer satisfaction.

Outcome

Dimensionality reduction uncovers hidden relationships, such as:

- A cluster of premium products with high ratings.

- Low-priced products frequently bought together.

12.5 Advantages and Limitations of Dimensionality Reduction

Advantages

1. **Improves Model Efficiency**: Reduces computational costs by eliminating redundant features.

2. **Enhances Interpretability**: Simplifies complex datasets for better understanding.

3. **Supports Visualization**: Allows visualization of high-dimensional data in two or three dimensions.

Limitations

1. **Loss of Information**: Some details may be lost during the reduction process.

2. **Parameter Sensitivity**: Techniques like t-SNE require careful parameter tuning.

3. **Black Box Nature**: Feature extraction methods can obscure the original data's meaning.

Dimensionality reduction is an essential technique for handling high-dimensional datasets. PCA and t-SNE, while serving different purposes, are powerful tools for simplifying and visualizing data. In this chapter, we explored their mechanics, applications, and limitations, and applied these methods to an e-commerce dataset.

Chapter 13: Text Mining and Sentiment Analysis

13.1 Text Preprocessing in R

Text data, also known as unstructured data, requires significant preprocessing to make it suitable for analysis. This involves cleaning, tokenization, and transforming the text into a structured format for further exploration. Let's dive into the essential steps of text preprocessing in R, using practical examples.

13.1.1 Understanding Text Data

Text data is ubiquitous in the form of customer reviews, tweets, emails, or documents. However, raw text is not immediately usable for analysis because:

- It often contains noise, such as punctuation, special characters, or irrelevant words.

- Words are in various forms (e.g., plurals, conjugations) that need standardization.

- The data may have stopwords—common words like "the," "and," or "but"—that don't add value to the analysis.

Example: A sample customer review:

arduino

"This is an amazing product! I've been using it for weeks, and it works perfectly."

13.1.2 Steps in Text Preprocessing

Here's a structured pipeline for text preprocessing in R:

1. **Loading and Inspecting the Data** Use readr to load text data and inspect its structure:

R

```
library(readr)

reviews <- read_csv("customer_reviews.csv")

head(reviews)
```

2. **Cleaning Text**

   - **Convert to Lowercase**: Ensures uniformity for case-sensitive operations.

   - **Remove Punctuation**: Eliminates unnecessary symbols.

- o **Remove Numbers**: Strips digits unless numeric data is relevant.
- o **Strip Whitespace**: Cleans up extra spaces.

Use the tm package to clean text:

R

```
library(tm)
clean_text <- tolower(reviews$text)
clean_text <- removePunctuation(clean_text)
clean_text <- removeNumbers(clean_text)
clean_text <- stripWhitespace(clean_text)
```

3. **Tokenization** Tokenization splits text into individual components such as words or sentences. The tidytext package simplifies this process:

R

```
library(tidytext)
tokens <- reviews %>%
  unnest_tokens(word, text)
```

4. **Stopword Removal** Common stopwords are removed to focus on meaningful words. Use predefined stopword lists from the stopwords package:

R

```r
library(stopwords)
tokens <- tokens %>%
  anti_join(stop_words, by = "word")
```

5. **Stemming and Lemmatization**
   - **Stemming** reduces words to their base or root form (e.g., "running" to "run").
   - **Lemmatization** achieves similar results but considers the context.

The SnowballC package provides stemming:

R

```r
library(SnowballC)
tokens$word <- wordStem(tokens$word)
```

6. **Creating a Document-Term Matrix (DTM)** A DTM represents text data in a tabular format with rows as documents and columns as terms:

R

```r
dtm <-
DocumentTermMatrix(Corpus(VectorSource(tokens$word)))
```

13.1.3 Tools for Text Preprocessing

- **tm**: Provides utilities for cleaning and preparing text.

- **tidytext**: Integrates text analysis into tidy data workflows.

- **textclean**: Handles text cleaning operations like handling contractions and misspellings.

13.2 Case Study: Analyzing Customer Reviews for Sentiment

Now that we've discussed the preprocessing pipeline, let's analyze customer reviews to determine their sentiment. Sentiment analysis identifies the emotional tone behind text, categorizing it as positive, negative, or neutral.

13.2.1 Problem Statement

A company collects customer feedback to understand user satisfaction and identify improvement areas. They want to:

1. Measure overall customer sentiment.

2. Identify frequent themes or complaints in negative reviews.

13.2.2 Dataset Description

For this case study, we use a dataset of 1,000 customer reviews with two columns:

- review_id: A unique identifier for each review.
- text: The text of the review.

13.2.3 Preprocessing the Data

We preprocess the text data following the steps outlined earlier:

1. Load the data:

R

```
reviews <- read_csv("customer_reviews.csv")
```

2. Clean the text:

R

```
reviews$text <- tolower(reviews$text) %>%
  removePunctuation() %>%
  removeNumbers() %>%
  stripWhitespace()
```

13.2.4 Lexicon-Based Sentiment Analysis

Lexicon-based methods use predefined dictionaries to assign sentiment scores to words. For this, we use the bing sentiment lexicon from the tidytext package.

1. **Join Words with Sentiment Lexicon**

R

```
sentiment_scores <- tokens %>%
  inner_join(get_sentiments("bing"), by = "word")
```

2. **Aggregate Sentiment Scores by Review**

R

```
sentiment_summary <- sentiment_scores %>%
  group_by(review_id) %>%
  summarize(sentiment = sum(sentiment_score))
```

3. **Classify Reviews**

   o Positive: Sentiment score > 0

   o Negative: Sentiment score < 0

   o Neutral: Sentiment score = 0

13.2.5 Visualizing Sentiment Distribution

Visualizations help understand overall trends. Use ggplot2 to create a histogram of sentiment scores:

R

```
library(ggplot2)

ggplot(sentiment_summary, aes(x = sentiment)) +

  geom_histogram(binwidth = 1, fill = "blue", color =
"black") +

  labs(title = "Sentiment Distribution of Customer
Reviews", x = "Sentiment Score", y = "Frequency")
```

13.2.6 Word Clouds for Positive and Negative Reviews

Word clouds visualize frequently occurring words. Create separate word clouds for positive and negative sentiments:

R

```
library(wordcloud)

positive_words <- tokens %>%

  filter(sentiment_score > 0) %>%

  count(word, sort = TRUE)

wordcloud(words = positive_words$word, freq =
positive_words$n, max.words = 100)


negative_words <- tokens %>%

  filter(sentiment_score < 0) %>%
```

```r
count(word, sort = TRUE)
```

```r
wordcloud(words = negative_words$word, freq =
negative_words$n, max.words = 100)
```

13.2.7 Advanced: Topic Modeling

To identify themes in negative reviews, apply Latent
Dirichlet Allocation (LDA) using the topicmodels
package:

R

```r
library(topicmodels)
dtm <-
DocumentTermMatrix(Corpus(VectorSource(tokens$
word)))
lda <- LDA(dtm, k = 5, control = list(seed = 123))
topics <- tidy(lda, matrix = "beta")
top_terms <- topics %>%
  group_by(topic) %>%
  top_n(10, beta) %>%
  arrange(topic, -beta)
```

Visualize the top terms for each topic:

R

```
ggplot(top_terms, aes(x = reorder(term, beta), y =
beta, fill = topic)) +

  geom_col(show.legend = FALSE) +

  facet_wrap(~ topic, scales = "free") +

  coord_flip() +

  labs(title = "Top Terms in Each Topic", x = "Terms",
y = "Beta")
```

In this chapter, we explored text preprocessing
techniques in R, including cleaning, tokenization, and
creating a document-term matrix. Using a case study
on customer reviews, we performed sentiment
analysis and uncovered actionable insights. By
combining lexicon-based methods and advanced
techniques like topic modeling, we demonstrated how
R can handle complex text data efficiently.

Chapter 14: Building Recommender Systems

14.1 Introduction to Recommender Systems

Recommender systems are algorithms designed to suggest items to users based on their preferences, behaviors, or the behaviors of similar users. They are central to many modern applications, from e-commerce websites suggesting products to users to streaming platforms recommending movies or music.

14.1.1 What are Recommender Systems?

In essence, a recommender system answers two primary questions:

- **What should we suggest to this user?**

- **How do we prioritize these suggestions?**

Recommender systems can be broadly categorized into two main approaches:

1. **Collaborative Filtering**: Leverages the preferences of similar users.

2. **Content-Based Filtering**: Focuses on the characteristics of the items and the user's historical preferences.

14.1.2 Importance of Recommender Systems

- **User Engagement**: Personalized recommendations increase user satisfaction and engagement.

- **Revenue Generation**: Platforms like Amazon and Netflix rely on these systems to boost sales or subscriptions.

- **Discovery**: They help users explore content they may not have found otherwise.

14.2 Collaborative Filtering Techniques

Collaborative filtering uses the collective behaviors or preferences of a group of users to recommend items.

14.2.1 User-Based Collaborative Filtering

In this method, users who have similar preferences are identified. For instance:

- If Alice and Bob have both liked *Movie A* and *Movie B*, and Alice also likes *Movie C*, we might recommend *Movie C* to Bob.

Steps:

1. Compute similarity between users using metrics like Pearson correlation or cosine similarity.

2. Identify the top N similar users.

3. Aggregate their preferences to generate recommendations.

14.2.2 Item-Based Collaborative Filtering

Rather than focusing on user similarity, this method identifies items that are often rated similarly. For example:

- If *Movie A* and *Movie B* are frequently rated by the same users, someone who likes *Movie A* is likely to enjoy *Movie B*.

Steps:

1. Compute similarity between items using correlation or cosine similarity.

2. Identify similar items for the user's past preferences.

3. Recommend items with high similarity scores.

14.2.3 Challenges in Collaborative Filtering

- **Cold Start Problem**: Difficulty in recommending for new users or items with insufficient data.

- **Scalability**: Computational challenges with large datasets.

- **Data Sparsity**: Many users only rate a small subset of items.

14.3 Content-Based Filtering Techniques

Content-based filtering relies on the attributes or metadata of items. For instance:

- If a user enjoys action movies, the system will recommend other action movies based on movie genres, actors, or directors.

14.3.1 How It Works

1. Extract features of items (e.g., genres, actors, or keywords for movies).

2. Create a user profile summarizing the features of items they've liked.

3. Recommend items that are most similar to the user profile.

14.3.2 Example of a Content-Based System

Consider a movie dataset:

- Attributes: Genre, director, cast, duration, etc.

- User preferences: Extracted from their viewing history.

Using similarity metrics such as cosine similarity or Euclidean distance, items similar to those already liked by the user are recommended.

14.3.3 Strengths and Weaknesses

- **Strengths**:
    - Can recommend niche items based on detailed user preferences.
    - Doesn't rely on the preferences of other users.

- **Weaknesses**:
    - Limited ability to recommend diverse items.
    - Suffers from the "serendipity problem," where it fails to recommend unexpected, interesting items.

14.4 Hands-On Project: Building a Movie Recommendation System

Let's implement a simple movie recommender system using R.

14.4.1 Dataset Description

For this project, we will use the **MovieLens** dataset, a popular dataset for building recommendation systems. It contains:

- User ratings for movies (on a scale of 1-5).
- Metadata about movies (e.g., genres, release year).

14.4.2 Step 1: Loading the Data

Start by loading the required libraries and importing the dataset:

R

```
# Load libraries
library(dplyr)
library(ggplot2)
library(recommenderlab)


# Load dataset (Assume MovieLens data is in a CSV format)
ratings <- read.csv("ratings.csv")
movies <- read.csv("movies.csv")


# Explore the data
head(ratings)
head(movies)
```

14.4.3 Step 2: Data Preprocessing

Clean and merge the datasets to prepare them for analysis:

R

```
# Merge movies and ratings
data <- merge(ratings, movies, by = "movieId")


# Check for missing values
summary(data)


# Filter for active users (users with sufficient ratings)
active_users <- data %>%
  group_by(userId) %>%
  filter(n() > 50)  # Keep users with >50 ratings
```

14.4.4 Step 3: Collaborative Filtering

Using the recommenderlab package, build a collaborative filtering model:

R

```
# Convert data into a recommenderlab matrix
rating_matrix <- as(data, "realRatingMatrix")
```

```r
# Create a User-Based Collaborative Filtering model
model_ubcf <- Recommender(rating_matrix, method
= "UBCF")


# Generate predictions for a specific user
recommendations <- predict(model_ubcf,
rating_matrix[1,], n = 5)
as(recommendations, "list")
```

14.4.5 Step 4: Content-Based Filtering

For content-based filtering, calculate item similarities:

R

```r
# Create a similarity matrix based on movie features
(genres, etc.)
similarity_matrix <- dist(movies[, c("genre",
"release_year")])


# Recommend similar movies based on a user's past
preferences
similar_movies <- movies[similarity_matrix[1,] < 0.5, ]
# Threshold = 0.5
head(similar_movies)
```

14.4.6 Step 5: Evaluation

Evaluate the performance of the recommender system using metrics such as precision, recall, or RMSE:

R

```
# Split the dataset into training and testing sets

train_data <- rating_matrix[1:800, ]

test_data <- rating_matrix[801:1000, ]


# Evaluate the collaborative filtering model

evaluation <- evaluationScheme(train_data, method = "split", train = 0.8)

model <- Recommender(train_data, method = "UBCF")

predictions <- predict(model, test_data, n = 5)


# Calculate accuracy metrics

accuracy <- calcPredictionAccuracy(predictions, test_data)

print(accuracy)
```

In this chapter, we explored the fundamentals of building recommender systems using collaborative and content-based filtering techniques. These systems have revolutionized the way we interact with digital platforms, offering highly personalized experiences. The hands-on project demonstrated how to build a movie recommender system in R, highlighting the key steps and challenges in implementation.

Chapter 15: Neural Networks and Deep Learning in R

15.1 Basics of Neural Networks and Deep Learning

15.1.1 What Are Neural Networks?

Neural networks are a subset of machine learning inspired by the structure and functioning of the human brain. They consist of layers of interconnected nodes (neurons) that process data in a way that allows the network to "learn" patterns and make predictions. Neural networks are particularly powerful for solving complex problems like image recognition, natural language processing, and more.

A typical neural network consists of:

1. **Input Layer**: Takes in raw data (e.g., pixel values for an image or numerical features).

2. **Hidden Layers**: Processes the data using a series of mathematical operations, transforming it into representations the network can understand.

3. **Output Layer**: Produces the final prediction or classification.

15.1.2 Key Concepts in Neural Networks

- **Weights and Biases**: Parameters that are adjusted during training to minimize error.

- **Activation Functions**: Introduce non-linearity to the model, enabling it to learn complex patterns. Examples include ReLU (Rectified Linear Unit), sigmoid, and tanh.

- **Loss Function**: Measures how well the network's predictions match the actual outcomes (e.g., mean squared error, cross-entropy).

- **Backpropagation**: An algorithm used to adjust weights by minimizing the error in predictions.

- **Epochs and Batches**: Training happens in multiple passes (epochs) over smaller subsets of data (batches).

15.1.3 Deep Learning

Deep learning refers to neural networks with many hidden layers, capable of modeling intricate relationships in large datasets. These networks are often used for tasks like image classification, speech recognition, and autonomous driving.

Deep learning in R is powered by libraries like **keras** and **tensorflow**.

15.2 Implementing Neural Networks in R

15.2.1 Setting Up the Environment

To work with deep learning in R, install the necessary libraries:

R

```r
install.packages("keras")
library(keras)
```

Install TensorFlow, the underlying framework:

R

```r
install_keras()
```

15.2.2 Building a Simple Neural Network

Let's create a basic neural network to classify data points into categories.

R

```r
# Generate some sample data
set.seed(42)
x <- matrix(runif(1000), nrow = 100)  # 100 samples,
10 features each
```

```r
y <- ifelse(rowSums(x) > 5, 1, 0)    # Binary labels
based on a threshold


# Split into training and test sets

train_x <- x[1:80, ]

test_x <- x[81:100, ]

train_y <- y[1:80]

test_y <- y[81:100]


# Define the model

model <- keras_model_sequential() %>%

  layer_dense(units = 10, activation = "relu",
input_shape = ncol(train_x)) %>%

  layer_dense(units = 5, activation = "relu") %>%

  layer_dense(units = 1, activation = "sigmoid")


# Compile the model

model %>% compile(

  optimizer = "adam",

  loss = "binary_crossentropy",

  metrics = c("accuracy")

)
```

```
# Train the model
history <- model %>% fit(
  train_x, train_y,
  epochs = 50,
  batch_size = 10,
  validation_split = 0.2
)


# Evaluate on test data
model %>% evaluate(test_x, test_y)
```

15.2.3 Interpreting Results

After training, the fit() function produces a history object that contains metrics like accuracy and loss. Use it to analyze training progress:

R

```
plot(history)
```

15.3 Real-World Application: Image Classification

15.3.1 Overview of Image Classification

Image classification is the task of assigning a label to an image. For example, recognizing whether a photo contains a cat or a dog. This is a fundamental deep learning application with extensive use cases in fields like healthcare (e.g., identifying tumors) and e-commerce (e.g., visual search).

15.3.2 Dataset Preparation

For this example, we'll use the **CIFAR-10** dataset, a collection of 60,000 32x32 color images in 10 categories (e.g., airplane, car, bird).

Load and preprocess the dataset:

R

```r
# Load CIFAR-10 dataset
cifar10 <- dataset_cifar10()

train_images <- cifar10$train$x / 255  # Normalize pixel values to 0-1

train_labels <- to_categorical(cifar10$train$y, num_classes = 10)

test_images <- cifar10$test$x / 255

test_labels <- to_categorical(cifar10$test$y, num_classes = 10)


# Check dimensions
dim(train_images)  # Should be 50000 x 32 x 32 x 3
```

15.3.3 Building the Model

A convolutional neural network (CNN) is ideal for image data due to its ability to capture spatial relationships.

R

```r
# Define CNN model
model <- keras_model_sequential() %>%
  layer_conv_2d(filters = 32, kernel_size = c(3, 3),
activation = "relu", input_shape = c(32, 32, 3)) %>%
  layer_max_pooling_2d(pool_size = c(2, 2)) %>%
  layer_conv_2d(filters = 64, kernel_size = c(3, 3),
activation = "relu") %>%
  layer_max_pooling_2d(pool_size = c(2, 2)) %>%
  layer_flatten() %>%
  layer_dense(units = 64, activation = "relu") %>%
  layer_dense(units = 10, activation = "softmax")  # 10
categories

# Compile the model
model %>% compile(
  optimizer = "adam",
  loss = "categorical_crossentropy",
  metrics = c("accuracy")
```

)

15.3.4 Training the Model

Train the model using the CIFAR-10 dataset:

R

```r
history <- model %>% fit(
  train_images, train_labels,
  epochs = 20,
  batch_size = 64,
  validation_split = 0.2
)
```

15.3.5 Evaluating the Model

Evaluate the model on test data:

R

```r
model %>% evaluate(test_images, test_labels)
```

Predict classes for new images:

R

```r
predictions <- model %>%
predict_classes(test_images[1:5, , , ])
print(predictions)
```

15.3.6 Visualizing Results

Display sample images along with predictions:

R

```
par(mfrow = c(1, 5))
for (i in 1:5) {
  plot(as.raster(test_images[i, , ]))
  title(paste("Prediction:", predictions[i]))
}
```

15.4 Challenges and Best Practices

15.4.1 Challenges in Neural Networks

1. **Overfitting**: When the model performs well on training data but poorly on unseen data.

   - **Solution**: Use regularization techniques (e.g., dropout layers) and collect more data.

2. **Computational Cost**: Training deep networks requires significant resources.

   - **Solution**: Use GPU-enabled systems or cloud-based tools like Google Colab.

3. **Data Quality**: Poor quality or imbalanced datasets can hinder model performance.

- o **Solution**: Preprocess and augment data to improve diversity.

15.4.2 Best Practices

- Start with simple models and progressively add complexity.

- Monitor performance metrics during training to detect overfitting early.

- Use cross-validation to ensure robustness.

This chapter introduced the basics of neural networks and deep learning in R, emphasizing their applications and practical implementation. By walking through an image classification example, you've learned how to preprocess data, build and train a CNN, and evaluate its performance.

Chapter 16: Deploying Machine Learning Models

16.1 Introduction to Model Deployment

Building a robust machine learning model is only part of the data science workflow. The ultimate goal is to make the model accessible and usable for stakeholders or end-users. Model deployment bridges the gap between developing a model and delivering its results in real-world applications.

What is Model Deployment?
Model deployment is the process of integrating a trained machine learning model into a production environment where it can make predictions or decisions based on real-time or batch inputs.

Why is Deployment Important?

- **Usability**: Models need to be accessible through user-friendly interfaces or APIs.

- **Scalability**: Deployment ensures that a model can handle large-scale or real-time data.

- **Integration**: Deployed models can be integrated into existing workflows or systems for continuous use.

Challenges in Deployment:

1. Ensuring model performance under production loads.

2. Handling changing data (data drift).

3. Providing a seamless interface for users.

R offers tools like **Shiny** and **Plumber** to simplify the deployment of machine learning models. This chapter focuses on packaging models into interactive web apps and APIs using these tools.

16.2 Packaging and Deploying Models with Shiny

Shiny is a web application framework for R that allows you to create interactive dashboards and apps. It's an excellent tool for deploying machine learning models where user interaction is required.

16.2.1 Basics of Shiny

A Shiny app has two primary components:

1. **UI (User Interface)**: Defines the layout and appearance of the app.

2. **Server**: Contains the logic for inputs, computations, and outputs.

16.2.2 Building a Shiny App

Here's an outline of how to use Shiny for model deployment:

1. **Install Shiny**:

R

```r
install.packages("shiny")
library(shiny)
```

2. **Create a Basic App**: A simple Shiny app is structured as follows:

R

```r
library(shiny)

ui <- fluidPage(
    titlePanel("Loan Approval Prediction"),
    sidebarLayout(
        sidebarPanel(
            numericInput("income", "Applicant Income:",
5000),
            numericInput("loan_amount", "Loan Amount:",
200),
            actionButton("predict", "Predict")
```

```r
  ),
  mainPanel(
    textOutput("result")
  )
 )
)


server <- function(input, output) {
  output$result <- renderText({
    paste("Prediction will appear here.")
  })
}


shinyApp(ui = ui, server = server)
```

3. **Enhancing with Model Integration**: Add a machine learning model to the server logic to make predictions based on user input.

4. **Run the App**: Save the code as app.R and run it with:

R

```r
shiny::runApp("app.R")
```

16.2.3 Integrating a Machine Learning Model

To deploy a machine learning model, follow these steps:

1. **Train the Model**: Use a dataset to train a model (e.g., logistic regression).

R

```R
model <- glm(approved ~ income + loan_amount, data = training_data, family = "binomial")
```

2. **Save the Model**: Save the trained model using saveRDS for later use.

R

```R
saveRDS(model, "loan_model.rds")
```

3. **Load and Use the Model in Shiny**: In the server logic, load the model and use it for predictions.

R

```R
model <- readRDS("loan_model.rds")

prediction <- predict(model, newdata = data.frame(income = input$income, loan_amount = input$loan_amount), type = "response")
```

4. **Display Results**: Render the prediction result dynamically in the UI.

16.3 Deploying Models with Plumber

While Shiny is ideal for interactive applications, Plumber is designed for creating APIs (Application Programming Interfaces). APIs allow models to be accessed programmatically by other systems or applications.

16.3.1 Basics of Plumber

Plumber transforms R functions into API endpoints, making it possible to expose machine learning models as RESTful APIs.

16.3.2 Building a Plumber API

1. **Install Plumber**:

R

```
install.packages("plumber")
library(plumber)
```

2. **Write an API Script**: Here's a basic Plumber script for a loan approval model:

R

```
library(plumber)


# Load the saved model
```

```r
model <- readRDS("loan_model.rds")


# Define the API endpoint
#* @post /predict
function(income, loan_amount) {
    new_data <- data.frame(income =
as.numeric(income), loan_amount =
as.numeric(loan_amount))
    prediction <- predict(model, newdata = new_data,
type = "response")
    ifelse(prediction > 0.5, "Approved", "Rejected")
}
```

3. **Run the API**: Save the script as plumber.R and run it with:

R

```r
library(plumber)
r <- plumb("plumber.R")
r$run(port = 8000)
```

4. **Access the API**: Test the API using tools like Postman or a web browser:

bash

http://localhost:8000/predict?income=5000&loan_amo
unt=200

16.3.3 Advantages of APIs:

- **Scalability**: Can handle requests from multiple users simultaneously.

- **Integration**: APIs can be used in web apps, mobile apps, or third-party tools.

- **Reusability**: Models can be reused across different platforms.

16.4 Example: Building a Loan Approval Web App

Let's combine the concepts of Shiny and a trained machine learning model into a complete web app for loan approval prediction.

1. **UI Design**: The app includes inputs for applicant income and loan amount, along with a button to submit the prediction request.

2. **Server Logic**: The server loads the pre-trained logistic regression model, processes inputs, and returns a prediction.

3. **Deploy the App**: After testing locally, deploy the app to a web hosting service like **ShinyApps.io**:

   - Create an account at ShinyApps.io.

- Install the rsconnect package:

R

```R
install.packages("rsconnect")
```

- Deploy the app:

R

```R
rsconnect::deployApp("path/to/app")
```

Code Example:

Here's a simplified version of the app:

R

```R
library(shiny)

# Load the pre-trained model
model <- readRDS("loan_model.rds")

# Define UI
ui <- fluidPage(
    titlePanel("Loan Approval Predictor"),
    sidebarLayout(
        sidebarPanel(
```

```r
        numericInput("income", "Applicant Income:",
5000),

        numericInput("loan_amount", "Loan Amount:",
200),

        actionButton("predict", "Predict")

      ),

      mainPanel(

        textOutput("result")

      )

    )

)


# Define server logic

server <- function(input, output) {

  observeEvent(input$predict, {

    income <- input$income

    loan_amount <- input$loan_amount

    new_data <- data.frame(income = income,
loan_amount = loan_amount)

    prediction <- predict(model, newdata =
new_data, type = "response")

    result <- ifelse(prediction > 0.5, "Approved",
"Rejected")

    output$result <- renderText(result)
```

```
  })

}
```

Run the app

```
shinyApp(ui = ui, server = server)
```

This chapter explored the deployment of machine learning models using Shiny for interactive web apps and Plumber for APIs. By deploying models, you can make your data science projects accessible and impactful in real-world applications. Whether building dashboards or providing programmatic APIs, R offers tools to bridge the gap between analysis and production.

Chapter 17: Handling Big Data in R

17.1 Introduction to Spark and Big Data Libraries

As data becomes increasingly voluminous, traditional data manipulation tools and techniques struggle to keep up. R, traditionally seen as a tool for small to medium-sized datasets, has adapted to meet the needs of big data processing through integration with tools like Apache Spark and specialized R libraries. This chapter explores how R tackles big data challenges effectively.

17.1.1 What is Big Data?

Big data refers to datasets that are too large, complex, or fast-changing to be efficiently processed using conventional tools. These datasets are often described using the 4 Vs:

1. **Volume**: The sheer size of data.

2. **Velocity**: The speed at which data is generated.

3. **Variety**: The diverse formats and types of data (structured, unstructured, or semi-structured).

4. **Veracity**: The uncertainty or inconsistency in the data.

Big data is ubiquitous across industries:

- **E-commerce**: Real-time analysis of customer behavior.

- **Healthcare**: Processing medical records for predictive analytics.

- **Finance**: Analyzing transaction data for fraud detection.

17.1.2 The Role of R in Big Data

R is inherently memory-bound, meaning it loads datasets into RAM for processing. While this works well for smaller datasets, it becomes impractical for big data. However, R's ecosystem offers several tools to bridge this gap:

- **Parallel Processing**: Splitting tasks across multiple CPU cores.

- **Out-of-Memory Processing**: Using disk storage to process datasets that don't fit in RAM.

- **Integration with Distributed Systems**: Using platforms like Apache Spark for distributed computation.

17.1.3 Introduction to Apache Spark

Apache Spark is a distributed computing framework designed for big data processing. Its key features include:

- **Speed**: In-memory computation makes Spark faster than traditional MapReduce.

- **Versatility**: Spark supports multiple programming languages, including R, and handles structured and unstructured data.

- **Scalability**: It scales seamlessly across large clusters of machines.

R integrates with Spark using the sparklyr package, which provides an intuitive interface to Spark's powerful distributed computing capabilities.

17.1.4 Big Data Libraries in R

1. **sparklyr**: A popular package that provides a seamless connection between R and Apache Spark.

2. **data.table**: Highly efficient for data manipulation with large datasets, although limited to single-machine use.

3. **ff**: Supports out-of-memory storage for datasets larger than RAM.

4. **bigmemory**: Provides tools to handle large matrices without exhausting system memory.

5. **dplyr with databases**: Connects directly to SQL databases for data manipulation without loading data into memory.

17.2 Real-World Application: Processing Large-Scale Transaction Data

To demonstrate R's capabilities for big data, let's walk through a case study involving the analysis of large-scale transaction data from an e-commerce company. The dataset consists of millions of transaction records, including details like timestamps, customer IDs, product IDs, and purchase amounts.

17.2.1 Setting Up Spark with R

1. **Install Sparklyr:**

R

```
install.packages("sparklyr")
```

2. **Connect to a Spark Session:**

R

```
library(sparklyr)
sc <- spark_connect(master = "local")
```

This initializes a local Spark session, suitable for prototyping and testing.

3. **Load the Data into Spark**: Use Spark's capabilities to handle large datasets:

R

```
transaction_data <- spark_read_csv(sc,

                name = "transactions",

                path =
"path/to/large_transaction_data.csv")
```

17.2.2 Data Profiling and Cleaning

Start by exploring the dataset to identify inconsistencies, missing values, and trends. Use Sparklyr's integration with dplyr for manipulation:

1. **Inspect Data**:

R

```
glimpse(transaction_data)
```

This provides an overview of the dataset's structure.

2. **Summary Statistics**:

R

```
transaction_data %>%
```

```
summarize(total_transactions = n(),

    avg_purchase = mean(purchase_amount),

    distinct_customers = n_distinct(customer_id))
```

3. **Handle Missing Data**: Replace missing values with appropriate substitutes:

R

```
transaction_data <- transaction_data %>%

  mutate(purchase_amount =
ifelse(is.na(purchase_amount), 0, purchase_amount))
```

17.2.3 Aggregation and Analysis

Perform high-level aggregations to uncover patterns:

1. **Daily Sales Trend**:

R

```
daily_sales <- transaction_data %>%

  mutate(date = as.Date(timestamp)) %>%

  group_by(date) %>%

  summarize(daily_revenue =
sum(purchase_amount))
```

2. **Customer Segmentation**: Group customers based on total spending:

R

```r
customer_segments <- transaction_data %>%
  group_by(customer_id) %>%
  summarize(total_spent = sum(purchase_amount)) %>%
  mutate(segment = case_when(
    total_spent >= 1000 ~ "High Value",
    total_spent >= 500 ~ "Medium Value",
    TRUE ~ "Low Value"
  ))
```

17.2.4 Visualizing Big Data Insights

After analysis, visualization is key to conveying findings. Use ggplot2 to create summaries:

1. **Visualize Daily Sales**:

R

```r
library(ggplot2)
ggplot(daily_sales, aes(x = date, y = daily_revenue)) +
  geom_line() +
```

```r
labs(title = "Daily Revenue Trends", x = "Date", y =
"Revenue")
```

2. **Visualize Customer Segments**:

R

```r
ggplot(customer_segments, aes(x = segment, y =
total_spent)) +

  geom_boxplot() +

  labs(title = "Customer Segmentation", x =
"Segment", y = "Total Spending")
```

17.2.5 Saving Processed Data

Processed data can be saved back to a storage
system for future use:

R

```r
spark_write_csv(transaction_data, path =
"path/to/processed_data")
```

17.3 Best Practices for Handling Big Data in R

1. **Use Chunk Processing**: When not using Spark, process data in chunks using readr or the ff package.

2. **Leverage Cloud and Distributed Systems**: Use cloud storage like AWS S3 in conjunction with Spark or Hadoop for large-scale operations.

3. **Optimize Code Efficiency**: Avoid loading unnecessary columns or rows, and use vectorized operations whenever possible.

4. **Monitor Resource Usage**: Keep track of memory and CPU usage to prevent crashes when dealing with big data.

This chapter introduced the challenges of big data and how R integrates with tools like Apache Spark to address them. Through a real-world case study, you learned how to process large-scale transaction data, from setup and data cleaning to aggregation and visualization. By combining R's flexibility with big data tools, you can tackle datasets of virtually any size while maintaining efficiency and clarity in your workflows.

Chapter 18: Ethical Considerations in Data Science

18.1 The Importance of Ethics in Data Science

Data science is not just about analyzing numbers or building models; it is also about making responsible and ethical decisions. The insights derived from data have far-reaching impacts, influencing business decisions, public policy, healthcare, and more. With great power comes great responsibility, and data scientists must approach their work with a strong ethical foundation.

What Makes Ethics Crucial in Data Science?

1. **Trust**: Ethical practices foster trust among users, stakeholders, and the general public.

2. **Fairness**: Ensures that algorithms and decisions do not discriminate against any group.

3. **Legal Compliance**: Adhering to laws like GDPR, HIPAA, and others ensures organizations avoid penalties.

4. **Sustainability**: Ethical practices contribute to the long-term viability of data-driven initiatives.

18.2 Data Privacy

Data privacy involves safeguarding the personal information of individuals and ensuring it is used only for its intended purposes. In the data science context, this is both a technical and moral imperative.

18.2.1 What is Data Privacy?

Data privacy refers to protecting personal data, such as names, addresses, medical records, and browsing habits, from unauthorized access and misuse. This protection is critical as organizations collect increasingly vast amounts of data.

18.2.2 Challenges in Ensuring Data Privacy

1. **Data Breaches**: Cyberattacks can compromise sensitive information.

2. **Unintended Inference**: Models may inadvertently reveal private details, such as identifying individuals in anonymized datasets.

3. **Overcollection of Data**: Gathering unnecessary data increases risk and raises ethical concerns.

4. **Global Regulations**: Laws like GDPR (General Data Protection Regulation) and

CCPA (California Consumer Privacy Act) vary across regions, adding complexity.

18.2.3 Best Practices for Data Privacy

1. **Anonymization**: Strip datasets of personal identifiers like names or addresses.

2. **Encryption**: Secure data both at rest and in transit using encryption techniques.

3. **Minimal Data Collection**: Collect only what is necessary for the specific purpose.

4. **User Consent**: Always obtain clear consent from individuals before collecting their data.

5. **Transparency**: Inform users how their data will be used and stored.

18.3 Bias in Data Science

Bias occurs when certain groups are unfairly advantaged or disadvantaged by data collection, analysis, or model predictions. Addressing bias is one of the most critical ethical challenges in data science.

18.3.1 Types of Bias in Data Science

1. **Data Bias**: Arises from non-representative or incomplete datasets.

   - Example: A facial recognition dataset that underrepresents certain ethnicities may lead to inaccurate results for those groups.

2. **Algorithmic Bias**: Occurs when machine learning models amplify biases present in the training data.

3. **Cognitive Bias**: Reflects human biases in interpreting or framing data.

18.3.2 Consequences of Bias

1. **Discrimination**: Marginalized groups may face unfair treatment, such as being denied loans or employment.

2. **Reputational Damage**: Bias can lead to public backlash and loss of trust.

3. **Legal Implications**: Bias-related decisions may violate anti-discrimination laws.

18.3.3 Mitigating Bias in Data Science

1. **Diverse Data**: Use datasets that are representative of the target population.

2. **Bias Testing**: Regularly evaluate models for biased outcomes using fairness metrics.

3. **Human Oversight**: Combine automated decision-making with human judgment.

4. **Algorithm Auditing**: Periodically audit algorithms for ethical compliance.

5. **Bias-Reduction Techniques**: Employ techniques like reweighting data or adversarial debiasing.

18.4 Responsible AI

Responsible AI ensures that artificial intelligence systems are fair, accountable, and transparent. It extends beyond technical accuracy to include ethical considerations in the design, deployment, and use of AI systems.

18.4.1 Principles of Responsible AI

1. **Fairness**: Avoid discrimination in AI outputs.

2. **Accountability**: Ensure organizations and individuals can be held accountable for AI-driven decisions.

3. **Transparency**: Make AI decision-making processes understandable to users.

4. **Safety**: Ensure that AI systems operate reliably and securely.

5. **Inclusivity**: Engage diverse stakeholders in AI development to prevent narrow perspectives.

18.4.2 Implementing Responsible AI

- Incorporate fairness constraints during model training.

- Provide clear explanations for AI decisions (e.g., using SHAP or LIME for interpretability).

- Conduct stakeholder reviews to ensure decisions align with societal values.

18.5 Case Study: Avoiding Bias in Hiring Algorithms

Hiring algorithms are increasingly used by companies to screen candidates, evaluate resumes, and predict job performance. However, these algorithms can unintentionally perpetuate bias, leading to discriminatory outcomes.

18.5.1 The Problem

Consider a company that uses an AI-powered hiring algorithm. The model is trained on historical hiring data, which reflects the company's past decisions. If the company has historically hired more men than women for technical roles, the algorithm may learn to favor male candidates, regardless of their actual qualifications.

18.5.2 Steps to Avoid Bias

1. **Identify Sources of Bias**

   o Analyze the training dataset for imbalances (e.g., gender, ethnicity, or age disparities).

   o Examine whether features like university attended or gaps in employment correlate with bias.

2. **Rebalance the Dataset**

- o Use oversampling or undersampling techniques to ensure all groups are equally represented.

- o Example: Augment the dataset with resumes from underrepresented groups.

3. **Feature Selection**

- o Remove features that may indirectly introduce bias (e.g., using zip code as a proxy for socioeconomic status).

- o Normalize features to prevent certain attributes from overpowering the model.

4. **Apply Fairness Metrics**

- o Evaluate the model using fairness metrics like disparate impact ratio or equal opportunity difference.

- o Example: Ensure the hiring rate for women and men with similar qualifications is comparable.

5. **Human Oversight**

- o Include human reviewers to validate AI-driven decisions.

- o Provide training for HR staff to understand AI outputs and ensure fairness.

6. **Continuous Monitoring**

- o Regularly audit the model to ensure its decisions remain unbiased over time.

- Example: Check for changes in demographic hiring patterns every quarter.

18.5.3 Results

By implementing these strategies, the company ensures that its hiring process is fair, transparent, and aligned with legal and ethical standards. Employees feel more confident that they are judged based on merit, fostering a more inclusive workplace culture.

18.6 Building an Ethical Culture in Data Science

Ethical practices go beyond technical fixes; they require a shift in organizational culture. Here are some steps to build an ethical culture:

1. **Leadership Commitment**: Senior leaders must prioritize ethical considerations in data science projects.

2. **Ethics Committees**: Establish a team to review and guide ethical practices in AI development.

3. **Training and Awareness**: Provide training for data scientists on ethical practices, including real-world scenarios.

4. **Stakeholder Engagement**: Involve diverse stakeholders, including ethicists, domain

experts, and affected communities, in decision-making.

5. **Documentation**: Maintain detailed records of datasets, algorithms, and decision-making processes to enhance accountability.

Ethical considerations in data science are not optional—they are essential. Data privacy, bias, and responsible AI are critical areas where data scientists must exercise caution and responsibility. By adhering to best practices and fostering an ethical culture, organizations can build trust, ensure fairness, and drive positive societal impact.

Chapter 19: Building Dashboards with Shiny

Dashboards are an essential tool for modern data communication. They allow users to interact with data, gain insights at a glance, and make data-driven decisions without needing programming expertise. In this chapter, we will explore how to build interactive dashboards using **Shiny**, a web application framework for R. We'll also walk through a real-world project: creating a **Sales Analytics Dashboard**.

19.1 What is Shiny?

Shiny is a package in R that enables users to build interactive web applications straight from R scripts. With Shiny, you can turn data analyses into dashboards or interactive applications without needing advanced web development skills. It bridges the gap between data and decision-making by providing an easy-to-use interface for non-technical stakeholders.

Key Features of Shiny

- **Interactivity**: Users can interact with data via sliders, dropdowns, buttons, and more.

- **Reactive Programming**: Automatically updates outputs when inputs change.

- **Customizability**: Allows for custom HTML, CSS, and JavaScript to enhance the dashboard.

- **Ease of Deployment**: Deploy your apps to Shiny Server, RStudio Connect, or even as standalone applications.

19.2 Creating Interactive Data Visualizations

Interactive dashboards with Shiny rely on two core principles:

1. **Reactive Inputs and Outputs**: Changes in user inputs dynamically update the outputs (e.g., charts or tables).

2. **Server-Client Architecture**: Shiny apps consist of a **UI (User Interface)** and a **server** function that handles the app's logic.

19.2.1 The Structure of a Shiny App

A basic Shiny app consists of three components:

1. **UI Function**: Defines how the app looks (layout, inputs, outputs).

2. **Server Function**: Contains the logic for processing inputs and generating outputs.

3. **App Call**: A call to shinyApp() to run the app.

Here's a simple example:

R

```r
library(shiny)

# UI function
ui <- fluidPage(
  titlePanel("Simple Shiny App"),
  sidebarLayout(
    sidebarPanel(
      sliderInput("num", "Choose a number:", min = 1, max = 100, value = 50)
    ),
    mainPanel(
      textOutput("result")
    )
  )
)

# Server function
server <- function(input, output) {
```

```
output$result <- renderText({

  paste("You selected:", input$num)

})

}
```

```
# Run the app

shinyApp(ui = ui, server = server)
```

19.2.2 Adding Interactive Visualizations

Visualizations in Shiny are dynamic and can respond to user inputs. For instance:

R

```
output$plot <- renderPlot({

  ggplot(mtcars, aes(x = hp, y = mpg)) +

    geom_point() +

    xlim(0, input$hp_limit)

})
```

By linking xlim() to a user-controlled slider (input$hp_limit), the chart updates based on the selected range.

19.3 Real-World Project: Sales Analytics Dashboard

To bring everything together, let's create a **Sales Analytics Dashboard**. This dashboard will allow users to:

1. Filter sales data by date range, region, or product category.

2. View summary statistics and trends.

3. Visualize sales performance through interactive charts.

19.3.1 Step 1: Preparing the Dataset

For this example, let's assume we have a CSV file called sales_data.csv with the following columns:

- Date: Transaction date.

- Region: Sales region.

- Product: Product category.

- Sales: Total sales amount.

- Units Sold: Number of units sold.

We'll load and preprocess the data in R:

R

```
sales_data <- read.csv("sales_data.csv")
```

```R
sales_data$Date <- as.Date(sales_data$Date, format = "%Y-%m-%d")
```

19.3.2 Step 2: Designing the User Interface

We'll use fluidPage() to organize the dashboard's layout. The UI will include:

- A sidebar for filters (date range, region, product).

- A main panel for displaying charts and tables.

Here's the initial UI code:

R

```R
ui <- fluidPage(
  titlePanel("Sales Analytics Dashboard"),
  sidebarLayout(
    sidebarPanel(
      dateRangeInput("date_range", "Select Date Range:", start = min(sales_data$Date), end = max(sales_data$Date)),
      selectInput("region", "Select Region:", choices = unique(sales_data$Region), selected = "All", multiple = TRUE),
      selectInput("product", "Select Product Category:", choices = unique(sales_data$Product), selected = "All", multiple = TRUE)
```

```
  ),
  mainPanel(

   tabsetPanel(

     tabPanel("Summary",
verbatimTextOutput("summary")),

     tabPanel("Sales Trends",
plotOutput("sales_trend")),

     tabPanel("Data Table",
tableOutput("filtered_data"))

    )

   )

  )

)
```

19.3.3 Step 3: Implementing Server Logic

The server logic processes user inputs, filters the dataset, and generates outputs.

1. Filtering Data Based on User Inputs

R

```
server <- function(input, output) {
  filtered_data <- reactive({
    data <- sales_data
```

```r
  if (!is.null(input$date_range)) {

    data <- data[data$Date >= input$date_range[1] &
data$Date <= input$date_range[2], ]

  }

  if ("All" %in% input$region == FALSE) {

    data <- data[data$Region %in% input$region, ]

  }

  if ("All" %in% input$product == FALSE) {

    data <- data[data$Product %in% input$product, ]

  }

  return(data)

 })

}
```

2. Generating Summary Statistics

R

```r
output$summary <- renderPrint({

  data <- filtered_data()

  summary(data)

})
```

3. Creating Sales Trend Visualizations

R

```
output$sales_trend <- renderPlot({

  data <- filtered_data()

  ggplot(data, aes(x = Date, y = Sales, color =
Region)) +

    geom_line() +

    labs(title = "Sales Trends Over Time", x = "Date", y
= "Sales")

})
```

4. Displaying the Filtered Data Table

R

```
output$filtered_data <- renderTable({

  filtered_data()

})
```

19.3.4 Step 4: Enhancing the Dashboard

To make the dashboard more user-friendly, consider
adding:

- **Interactive Plots**: Use the plotly package for
  zoomable, hoverable charts.

- **KPIs (Key Performance Indicators)**: Add
  boxes showing total sales, average sales, etc.

- **Custom Styling**: Use CSS or the shinythemes package for a polished look.

19.3.5 Deploying the Dashboard

Shiny apps can be deployed in several ways:

1. **Run Locally**: Share the R script and dataset with others who have R installed.

2. **Shiny Server**: Host the app on a server for remote access.

3. **RStudio Connect**: Deploy with advanced collaboration features.

4. **shinyapps.io**: Deploy to RStudio's cloud-hosting service with minimal setup.

R

```
rsconnect::deployApp("path/to/app_directory")
```

Building dashboards with Shiny transforms static analyses into interactive experiences, empowering users to explore data intuitively. By integrating user inputs, reactive visualizations, and real-world data, you can create dynamic tools tailored to your audience's needs.

The **Sales Analytics Dashboard** we built in this chapter serves as a foundational template for creating advanced dashboards. Experiment with additional features, such as drill-downs or predictive analytics, to enhance functionality.

Chapter 20: The Future of Data Science with R

20.1 Emerging Trends in Data Science and R's Role

Data science is evolving at an unprecedented pace, with new trends and technologies emerging regularly. As a versatile and open-source programming language, R remains well-positioned to adapt and thrive in this dynamic landscape. Let's explore the key trends shaping the future of data science and how R is poised to play a vital role.

20.1.1 Trend 1: The Rise of Automated Machine Learning (AutoML)

Automated Machine Learning (AutoML) tools are simplifying the process of building, tuning, and deploying machine learning models. These tools allow data scientists to focus on the problem at hand rather than manual feature engineering and parameter tuning.

- **R's Role**: R has embraced AutoML through packages like caret, mlr3, and h2o. These tools automate model selection, hyperparameter tuning, and performance evaluation, making machine learning workflows more efficient.

20.1.2 Trend 2: Growth in Explainable AI (XAI)

As machine learning models become more complex, the need for transparency and interpretability grows. Explainable AI ensures that stakeholders can trust the outputs of these models.

- **R's Role**: R offers packages like DALEX and lime to visualize and interpret machine learning models. These tools provide insights into feature importance and model behavior, aligning with the demand for explainability.

20.1.3 Trend 3: Data Science for Sustainability

Organizations are leveraging data science to address global challenges such as climate change, resource optimization, and sustainable development. Predictive analytics and simulations are helping create actionable solutions.

- **R's Role**: R is extensively used in environmental research and sustainability projects. Packages like raster and sf enable geospatial analysis, crucial for studying climate patterns and resource management.

20.1.4 Trend 4: Integration with Big Data and Cloud Platforms

The rise of big data technologies and cloud computing has transformed how data is stored, processed, and analyzed. Cloud-based solutions provide scalable infrastructure for handling massive datasets.

- **R's Role**: R integrates seamlessly with big data platforms like Apache Spark (via sparklyr) and cloud services like AWS and Google Cloud. These integrations allow data scientists to process large-scale data efficiently.

20.1.5 Trend 5: Data Democratization

The future of data science involves empowering non-technical users to leverage data-driven insights. Tools and languages that simplify data workflows are becoming essential.

- **R's Role**: With its robust visualization capabilities (ggplot2, Shiny), R allows even non-programmers to create intuitive dashboards and interactive applications. This democratization fosters a data-driven culture within organizations.

20.1.6 Trend 6: Emphasis on Ethical Data Science

Ethical considerations are becoming central to data science, focusing on reducing biases, ensuring privacy, and promoting fairness in AI systems.

- **R's Role**: R supports ethical data practices with tools like fairmodels for fairness evaluation and privBayes for privacy-preserving data analysis. Its open-source nature also fosters transparency and collaboration.

20.2 Practical Advice for Career Development in Data Science

As the field of data science grows, so does the competition. Staying ahead requires a combination of technical expertise, strategic thinking, and continuous learning. Here's a roadmap for aspiring and experienced data scientists to excel in their careers.

20.2.1 Building a Strong Foundation

Success in data science starts with mastering the fundamentals. Aspiring professionals should focus on:

- **Statistical Knowledge**: A solid grasp of statistics is crucial for understanding data and building robust models.

- **Programming Skills**: Proficiency in R is a significant advantage due to its wide adoption in the data science community.

- **Data Wrangling and Visualization**: Skills in data manipulation (e.g., using dplyr) and visualization (e.g., using ggplot2) are indispensable.

20.2.2 Staying Updated with Emerging Tools and Techniques

The data science landscape is continuously evolving. To remain relevant:

- **Explore New Packages**: Stay informed about new R packages that streamline workflows or offer novel capabilities.

- **Learn Complementary Tools**: For example, understanding Python or SQL can expand your versatility as a data scientist.

- **Engage with the Community**: Follow blogs, forums, and conferences to stay current with industry trends.

20.2.3 Developing Domain Expertise

While technical skills are essential, domain knowledge differentiates good data scientists from great ones. Understanding the business or research context allows you to ask the right questions and develop impactful solutions.

- **How to Build Domain Expertise**:
  - Collaborate with domain experts on projects.

- o Read case studies and industry-specific literature.
- o Analyze publicly available datasets in your area of interest.

20.2.4 Building a Portfolio

A strong portfolio showcases your skills and experience to potential employers or clients. Include:

- **Projects**: Highlight projects that solve real-world problems using R.

- **Visualization Dashboards**: Create interactive visualizations or apps using Shiny.

- **GitHub Repository**: Share your code and collaborate with others.

20.2.5 Networking and Community Involvement

Building a professional network can open doors to new opportunities. Here's how to get started:

- **Join Online Communities**: Participate in R-specific forums (e.g., RStudio Community, Stack Overflow).

- **Attend Conferences**: Events like useR! and RStudio::conf are great for learning and networking.

- **Contribute to Open-Source Projects**: Enhance your skills and give back to the community by contributing to R packages.

20.2.6 Pursuing Continuous Learning

Data science is a journey, not a destination. Here are ways to keep learning:

- **Enroll in Advanced Courses**: Deepen your knowledge in machine learning, time series analysis, or geospatial analysis.

- **Read Books and Research Papers**: Stay informed about the latest methodologies and applications.

- **Experiment with New Data Sets**: Explore publicly available datasets to practice your skills.

20.2.7 Soft Skills for Data Scientists

Beyond technical prowess, successful data scientists possess strong communication and problem-solving abilities. Develop:

- **Storytelling Skills**: Learn to translate data insights into compelling narratives.

- **Collaboration Skills**: Work effectively with cross-functional teams, including engineers, analysts, and business leaders.

20.3 The Future of R in Data Science

While Python has gained popularity in recent years, R continues to be a critical tool in the data science ecosystem. Here's why R will remain relevant in the future:

20.3.1 Specialization in Statistics and Research

R's roots in statistics make it indispensable for advanced statistical modeling and research-focused analysis. Fields like biostatistics, epidemiology, and social sciences heavily rely on R.

20.3.2 Expanding Libraries and Tools

The R community consistently develops new libraries to address emerging challenges. For example:

- **tidymodels**: A modern approach to machine learning.

- **sf and terra**: For geospatial data analysis.

- **text2vec**: For natural language processing.

20.3.3 Integration with Emerging Technologies

R's compatibility with big data tools (e.g., Hadoop, Spark) and cloud platforms ensures its adaptability in large-scale and cloud-based analytics.

20.3.4 Collaboration with Other Languages

R's interoperability with Python, C++, and Java allows it to be part of diverse data science pipelines. Tools like reticulate enable seamless integration between R and Python.

The future of data science is bright, dynamic, and full of opportunities. R's role in this evolution is secure due to its statistical strengths, visualization capabilities, and adaptability to emerging technologies. By mastering R, staying curious, and continuously learning, you can build a thriving career in data science while contributing to impactful solutions in a data-driven world.

www.ingramcontent.com/pod-product-compliance
Lightning Source LLC
LaVergne TN
LVHW051330050326
832903LV00031B/3451